Entrepreneurship and Social Mobility

Bruno Grancelli

# Entrepreneurship and Social Mobility

## Two Cosmopolitan Lives in Renaissance Genoa

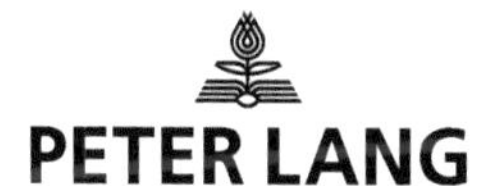

PETER LANG

**Bibliographic Information published by the
Deutsche Nationalbibliothek**
The Deutsche Nationalbibliothek lists this publication in the Deutsche
Nationalbibliografie; detailed bibliographic data is available online at
http://dnb.d-nb.de.


**Library of Congress Cataloging-in-Publication Data**
A CIP catalog record for this book has been applied for at the
Library of Congress.


ISBN 978-3-631-88487-4 (Print)
E-ISBN 978-3-631-88498-0 (E-PDF)
E-ISBN 978-3-631-88499-7 (EPUB)
10.3726/b19989

*To Mirella*

# Contents


Acknowledgments ....................................................... 9

Chapter One  Introduction ......................................... 11

Chapter Two  The city-state: A polity with a
transactional focus .............................................. 23

Chapter Three  Bartolomeo da
Framura: Manager on the alum fields ................... 43

3.1.  Merchant within a trading and ecclesiastical
network ........................................................ 43

3.2.  Contractor and trader in the Papal quarries
(1460–1466) ..................................................... 50

Chapter Four  Gioachino da Passano: Trusted
men of King Francis I .......................................... 57

4.1.  Merchant and commander of the galleys ............. 58

4.2.  Geopolitical strategist on the French side ........... 61

Chapter Five  Entrepreneurship and
institutions: Lessons from the case ....................... 67

5.1.  Notes on oligarchic closure and social mobility
in early modern Genoa ...................................... 70

8 Contents

**Chapter Six  Giving a historical face to entrepreneurship: Issues for debate** ...... 89

6.1. Historical thinking on entrepreneurship within the cultural turn ............... 90

6.2. Another way of reasoning .................... 98

**Chapter Seven  Summary and concluding remarks** ......................... 103

**Synopsis** .......................... 113

**References** ......................... 115

# Acknowledgments

At the origin of this study lies a collective research on the history of a Genoese *podesteria* which, in its four centuries of existence, always had a quite large group of nobles, merchants and navigators who made their careers in Genoa and beyond. Among the most notable of them, are the two characters depicted here with biographical sketches that benefited from the research skills of several scholars in different times and places. My thanks go in particular to Andrea Lercari, Ivana Ait and Diego Pizzorno. I am also grateful to the anonymous reviewer who provided very helpful comments and suggestions for my attempt to turn a descriptive case study into an interpretive one.

# Chapter One   Introduction

The archival research from which the present study originates is a multi-themed description of a Genoese *podesteria*,[1] from its documented existence in 1368 through the fall of the Republic of Genoa in 1797. A significant element of interest in that collective work is the theoretical potential that transpires from descriptions of the local socio-economic structure and its intersections with the capital city, the hegemonic role a noble family one of our actors belonged to exerted in the local community and other parts of the Genoese *dominio* and finally, the business of a bunch of local merchants in Genoa and beyond.[2]

---

1   A locality governed by a *podestà*. Several *podesterie* could be included in a captaincy *(capitanato)* as it happened to Framura, included into the captaincy of Levanto in 1636.

2   Specifically, the main drivers of the local socio-economic dynamism in the *podesteria* of Framura may be summarized as follows. First, the settlement of a noble family, in this and the adjacent small town of Levanto, which fulfilled a hegemonic role in the eastern part of the Genoese *dominio* since the twelfth century. Second, the command by the city government to ships of more than 20 registered tons to base their operations not on local moorings, but only in the port of Genoa. Third, the concession, under the Sforza's rule (1464–1478), of the right to exploit local mines of silver, iron and copper along with some marble quarries. Finally, the trade of valuable products, such as silkworms, but also wine, which granted the Framuresi a monopoly position in the dockyard of wine. The archival sources examined were: municipal resolutions; taxation of properties; property purchases, administration of the Marquis, court cases, baptisms, marriage contracts, wills, states of the souls and petitions to authorities of the Republic. The outcomes of the archival research of higher interest here are in, Andrea Lercari, "Una

In fact, such a descriptive case outlined a set of micro-level dynamics of a macro-process that got completed in late-medieval Genoa: the turning of its economic elite into a ruling class. That élite includes Bartolomeo da Framura and Gioachino da Passano, two cosmopolitan actors who will go from the role of merchants to that of "specialists" engaged in the implementations of strategic policies of princes and popes.[3] This is the reason why references in the literature may be found

comunità ligure di antico regime: personaggi e famiglie framuresi tra XV e XVIII secolo, " pp. 265–646, in A. Lercari (ed.), *Framura. Un'antica terra ligure fra il mare e i monti*, Genova, AGF, 2017; Barbara Bernabò, "La storia secolare di un territorio antico," in Lercari (2017), pp. 265–332; Giorgio Casanova, "Framura e il mare: una vocazione millenaria fra pescatori, naviganti e corsari," in Lercari (2017), pp. 857–923.

3  As Jacques Heers points out, the complex Genoese economy was not dominated and controller solely by merchants insofar as they had to rely on various kind of specialists and intermediaries such as technicians, business brokers, insurance and bank agents and, most of all, notaries. (*Genova nel '400. Civiltà mediterranea, grande capitalismo e capitalismo popolare*, Milano, Jaca Book, 1983, pp. 328–330). The primary sources on the two characters described in this case are the following. Jean Delumeau, *L'alun de Rome. XV-XIXe siècle*, Paris, S.E.V.P.E.N., 1962; Benjamin Weber, "Lutter contre le Turcs: Les formes nouvelles de la croisade pontificale au XVe siecle (l'alun de Tolfa)," *Collection de l'Ecole française de Rome*, no. 42, 2013, pp. 315–324; Ivana Ait, "Dal governo signorile al governo mercantile: i monti della Tolfa e le 'lumere' del papa," in *Mélanges de l'Ecole française de Rome-Moyen Age*, 126-1, 2014, pp. 1–59; Guillaume Alonge, "Evangelismo e ortodossia nella diplomazia franco-turca di Francesco I," *Melanges de l'Ecole française de Rome-Italie et Mediterrannée modernes et contemporaines*, 129-2, 2017; Andrea Lercari (ed.), I signori da Passano. Identità territoriale, grande politica e cultura europea nella storia di una antica stirpe del Levante ligure, vol. I and II, *Giornale Storico della Lunigiana e del Territorio Lucense*, 2009–2011. On

on these characters within the backdrop of two critical junctures in Genoese history. First, the withdrawal from the colonies in the Levant as a result of the Ottoman advance in the second half of the 15th century. Second, the positioning of the city-state within the Spanish imperial framework after Admiral Andrea Doria changed sides soon after his takeover of Genoa with the French support in 1528.[4]

The global lives of these upwardly mobile cosmopolitan actors seem a well-suited subject for reasoning on how "biography interacts with the history of [the subject's] era."[5] In the present work, the issue is defined and delimited by using the biography-history framework as a backdrop for reassessing the historical reasoning on entrepreneurship proposed by business historians who responded to the "Schumpeter's plea" in this regard.[6]

---

these two, and other 'glocal' actors, see, Bruno Grancelli, *Nobili, mercanti e navigatori framuresi. Azione economica, arte, diplomazia nel Secolo dei Genovesi*, Carrara, Impressum, 2019.

4   Arturo Pacini (1999), *La Genova di Andrea Doria nell'impero di Carlo V*: Firenze, Olschki; Gabriella Airaldi (2015), *Andrea Doria*, Salerno Editrice; Carlo Bitossi, 'L'età di Andrea Doria', in *Storia della Liguria*, in Giovanni Assereto and Marco Doria (eds.), Bari, Laterza, 2007, pp. 61–78; Bartolomé Yun Casalilla (2009), *Las Redes del Imperio. Elites sociales en la articulación de la Monarquía Hispánica,-1492-1714*, Madrid, Marcial Pons, 2009; Manuel Herrero Sanchez, Yasmina Rocio Ben Yessef Garcia, Carlo Bitossi, Dino Puncuh (2011) (eds.), *Genova y la Monarquia Hispanica (1528-1713)*, Atti della Società Ligure di Storia Patria, vol. LI (CXXV), Fasc. 1; Cristina Bravo Lozano, Roberto Quirós Rosado (eds.) (2013) *En Tierra de Confluencias. Italia y la Monarquia de España*, Roma, Albatros.

5   Lois W. Banner, "Biography as History," *American Historical Review*, vol. 114, no. 3, 2009, pp. 579–586.

6   For an overview of how business historians have responded to the Schumpeter's plea for a historical reasoning on entrepreneurship that goes farther back than the Industrial Revolution, see

The statement on the biography that "confirms a farewell to theory" is today disconfirmed. But what does the biographical perspective specifically add to our knowledge of the past? In his reply to the question, Hans Renders claims that the biographical method can strengthen "the shift from the abstract and structural approaches of the past to the situating of human experience as the starting point of historical interpretation." Thus, the use of primary sources and the personal perspective, within a microhistorical approach, should be the way to explore, relativize, confirm or correct the existing understandings and interpretations of the past.

Microhistory was indeed the backdrop of the archival research referred to above. Yet, its thick description has given reasons for trying to build an interpretive case in which what is situated is not an all-encompassing human experience. Rather, it is a middle-range form of agency whose social and institutional embeddedness requires some advancements in what seems to be difficult in microhistorical approaches.[7] In essence, the growing

---

R. Daniel Wadhwani and Christina Lubinski (2017), "Reinventing Entrepreneurial History," *Business History Review*, 91 (Winter 2017), pp. 767–799. The attempt proposed by the two authors is organized according to the following criteria. Analysis is not to be centred on actors, hierarchies, or institutions. Rather, the focus should shift on three specific aspects of the entrepreneurial process: envisioning and valuing opportunities, allocating and reconfiguring resources, and legitimizing novelty.

7   This kind of difficulty is explained by Jan de Vries in two essays: "Changing the Narrative: The New History That Was and Is to Come," *Journal of Interdisciplinary History*, 48, no. 3, 2017, pp. 313–334 and, "Playing with Scale: The Global and the Micro, the Macro and the Nano," *Past and Present*, vol. 42, issue supplement 14, 2019, pp. 23–36. The term "middle-range forms of agency" has been used by Kaarle Wirta in his analysis of

influence of microhistory brought about by the "biographical turn" has been based on two widespread beliefs. The history of an individual life, even the most obscure, can shed light on the past and the same applies to "new historical subjects" emerging from the various fields of social history.[8]

These research premises imply new methodologies. One is that of telling a complete and coherent story of an individual with the aim of examining how that subject carries out the process of self-invention. The other is part of a stream of research that refuses the tradition in the social history of studying "the top-down decision-making of Great Men [...] to uncover experience and impact of ordinary people"[9] In short, among the underpinning of the biographical research, there is a will to move away from structuralist approaches and explanations towards approaches more sensitive to the agency of individual and collective actors. The shift has been twofold. First, from the pre-eminence of class divisions to a concern about categories that cut across class boundaries (such as gender and ethnicity). Second, from "grand narratives" that privileged the views of dominant classes to a focus on subordinate groups and life stories to understand how

---

'Atlantic' entrepreneurs (see, *Early Modern Overseas Trade and Entrepreneurship. Nordic Trading Companies in the Seventeenth Century*, London, Routledge, 2020).

8    As for the first stance, the seminal works are: Carlo Ginsburg, *Il formaggio e i Vermi,* Torino, Einaudi, 1976 and, Giovanni Levi, *L'eredità immateriale. Carriera di un esorcista nel Piemonte del Seicento*, Milano, Il Saggiatore, 1985.The second stance is expressed in the growing literature on gender, race and class. For an overview see, for example, Adrian Shubert, "What Do Historians Really Think About Biography," *Letras de Hoje*, vol. 53, no. 2, 2018, pp. 96–102.

9    Ibid., p. 200.

they were affected by specific historical developments.[10] Still, this shift does not imply that the stories of "prominent individuals" are to be neglected. Rather, what is to be investigated as well in the microhistorical approach are the social and political circumstances "that enabled their rise to prominence and their exercise of power."[11]

Admittedly, these new approaches to biography in history come to terms with individual lives without neglecting the analysis of political institutions, social structures, and developments. But even these advances in the way to explore the changing nature of the history-biography link still rest on the idea that the focus should shift from the historical role of "Great Men" to how the lives of disempowered individuals mirror wide patterns of socio-institutional change.[12] Consequently, the claim for the reflective capacity of individual lives is made within a framework which leaves people who are empowered by the "Great Men" out of the picture. Our two characters represent such kind of individuals and cannot be easily included in these microhistorical approaches. Neither can they be included in global microhistory centred on people belonging to minorities who also act as cultural mediators as those of merchant diasporas.[13]

A reachable way to put agency in context is instead suggested by Jan de Vries, i.e., to study the global lives of "unusually

---

10  Barbara Caine, *Biography and History (Theory and History)*, Palgrave Macmillan, 2018, p. 2.

11  See, for instance, Maya Yasanoff, *The Dawn Watch. Joseph Conrad in a Global World*, Penguin, 2017.

12  Caine, 2018, p. 124.

13  See, among others, Francesca Trivellato, *The Familiarity of Strangers: The Sephardic Diaspora, Livorno and Cross-Cultural Trade in the Early Modern Period*, Yale University Press, 2009; Christian De Vito and Anne Geritsen (eds.), *Micro-Spatial Histories of Global Labour*, Palgrave Macmillan, 2018.

cosmopolitan individuals" to highlight global forces through the prism of individual experience.[14] The question de Vries put forward is whether these cosmopolitan actors may be considered peers of the "exceptional-typical" individual addressed in microhistory.[15] Somewhat they are, or at least they have been studied as such, but in general, "they seem inconsistent with microhistorical eschewal of elite biography and preference for the lives of people of little account in their society"[16] It is an inconsistency that de Vries explains with a lack of suitable methods to overcome it in the repertoire of microhistorians. These methods would be case studies whereby detailed intra-case descriptions of specific phenomena are coupled with comparisons of the same events in different contexts. In short, the case study approach should be linked with a more prospective scale of historical investigation in which the uncovering of connections among multiple evidences do not rule out the identification of causal processes of historical change. Thick descriptions have their own heuristic value but not within inward views that blur the differences between past and present and hinder the application of social-scientific standards to generalizations.[17]

The two examples of unusually cosmopolitan actors presented in this study show that the casing process to turn a thick description into an interpretive study cannot be pursued

---

14  See de Vries, "Playing with Scale", p. 27.

15  Exceptional-normal is the oxymoron used in microhistory to demonstrate the strategic paths that seemingly disempowered actors are able to devise and negotiate by taking advantage of incongruities among different normative systems. See, Edoardo Grendi, "Ripensare la microstoria?" *Quaderni Storici*, vol. 29, no. 86, 1994, pp. 539–549.

16  de Vries, 2019, p. 29.

17  Ibid., p. 30–31.

by accepting the research premises of microhistory outlined above. These local and then cosmopolitan actors, are upwardly mobile as well. Thus, a further step in setting the research design has been an assessment of the recent investigations on social mobility in late medieval and early modern Italy. Such an appraisal does not claim to be an exhaustive discussion of that stream of research . Rather, it represents the positions relevant to the aim of this study, that is, providing new insights into the historical reasoning on entrepreneurship in a period in which economic actors would often perform the functions of political entrepreneurs.

In the stream of mobility studies referred to here, the evidence on the social advancement of individuals and groups is compared and discussed around the thesis of "oligarchic closure," and whether or not entrepreneurship was stifled by that closure to the advantage of rent-seeking at the service of princes or state and communal authorities.[18] That debate, with its interdisciplinary bent, yielded some useful lessons for the choice of the approach to biography and history to apply in this study. First, it is to interrogate local sources on issues relating to the social actors focusing on them and their circles without it implying "little interest in elites and the propellants of power at home and abroad." It is also to not assume that "perceptions and dispositions possess an overwhelming power in directing human action while material conditions should be drastically downgraded." Second, it is to provide ways to sound out the spheres of action not only to search for what is typical, but also to catch the breadth and variations of life stories. And, through

---

18  See specifically, Sergio Tognetti, "Uomini d'affari e mobilità sociale in Italia tra metà Trecento e primo cinquecento," *Estratto da Archivio Storico Italiano*, 1-a. 175 n. 651, Firenze Olschki Editore, 2017, pp. 119–150.

comparative references, to specify "what spheres of action have existed for which individuals and the extent to which some of them have been able to fully encompass these spaces or even to transcend them."[19] Third, it is to comply with the quest for a certain degree of eclecticism to better conceptualize an agency and its relationships in shifting contexts and highlight the dynamics that fostered multiple identities of agents that did not break their localized links.[20]

This study is organized as follows. Chapter Two describes the main features of the initial setting whereby our characters found the springboard of their transprofessional and transnational careers. The first section sketches a picture that highlights why the polity of the city-state was typified by a transactional focus. By the mid-15th century, Genoa is going to dominate financial markets but remains ungovernable and ridden by factional fighting until a solution is found in the contracting out of government functions to the Bank of Saint George. The second section outlines the critical juncture of 1528–1576 when an attempt to build a centralized administrative structure such as those of other regional states met with only partial success. This time, the chronically weak enforcement capacities of the communal government proved more difficult to be overcame

---

19 Volker Berghahn, "Structuralism and Biography. Some Concluding Thoughts on the Uncertainties of a Historiographical Genre," p. 236, in Volker R. Berghahn and Simone Lassig (eds.), *Biography Between Structure and Agency, Central European Lives in International Historiography*, New York, Berghahn, 2008.

20 Sarah Panter, Johannes Paulmann and Margit Szöllösi-Janze, "Mobility and Biography: Methodological Challenges and Perspectives," p. 4, in Johannes Paulmann, Markus Friedrich, Nick Stargardt (eds.), *Jahrbuch für Europäische Geschichte / European History Yearbook* –Sarah Panter " (ed.), *Band 16. Mobility and Biography*, Berlin, de Gruyter, 2015, pp. 1–14.

in the "Feudal Mountain" than in the capital city. The chapter then also refers to another form of contracting out, this time in the domain of criminal justice: the "pacification agreements" between officials and local kinships that should have reined in their own troublemakers and street bandits.

The third chapter focuses on the dynamics of social advancement of Bartolomeo da Framura who started as a merchant, money lender, sailor and investor in real estate in the village which gave him his surname. It is a social advancement that gets a significant thrust in Genoa whereby he upgrades his network of social relations, becomes vice-chancellor in the Commune, and then contractor for the tax collection in Sardinia. Genoa is also the place whereby he makes the strategic choice of buying the post of "apostolic writer" of the Papal court. The chapter then describes how this character is going to reach the top of his transprofessional career in the aftermath of a critical juncture in which Genoa gradually loses its colonies in the Levant. The chapter concludes with an account of how the registrar of papal bulls turns into a mining entrepreneur in the alum fields in the Papal State that he had discovered along with two partners and will manage from 1460 through 1466.

Chapter Four focuses on the multivalent transnational career of Gioachino da Passano, a highly skilled negotiator who began by transacting on the price of grains in the Eastern part of the Genoese *dominio*. He then became a military commander to end up negotiating the liberation of prestigious hostages, such as Francis I of Valois, after his defeat in the second of the Italian wars (1499–1504). The first section outlines his earlier career path before the critical juncture of 1528 in which he decided to part company with Andrea Doria when the admiral decided to get Genoa embedded into the Spanish imperial framework. The second section describes the most important activities of this key actor in the geopolitical arena of his times and how he used his social capital and political clout to play a crucial role within the anti-Spanish diplomacy of Francis I.

Chapter Five aims to explicate the forms of agency of our upwardly mobile and cosmopolitan actors who played crucial roles in the implementation of policies on behalf of their "principals" in Genoa and beyond. It elaborates on some methodological insights that can be gleaned from the stream of researches on social mobility in Medieval and early modern Italy. This is being done by comparing and contrasting the two theses of "oligarchic closure" and the formation of an "urban proto-bourgeois class" with a focus on the hub of economic development and international trade that Genoa had been in the "Century of the Genoese". The chapter concludes with a comparative reference to studies on the coupling between directives and pressures of institutional actors and responses of their "assigned entrepreneurs" in organizational contexts such as those of some West India companies of the XVI and XVII centuries. These organization studies complement those on social mobility and are the third step to form an analytical vocabulary to turn a descriptive case into an interpretative one.

Chapter Six singles out some issues for debate in business history on giving a historical face to entrepreneurship in light of the lessons learned from the case study. Is it possible to think of the theme and neglect the structures in which economic action is going to unfold and translate into a political clout? Has the study of entrepreneurship really turned into a stifled alternative in business history? And assuming that to be true, is the way to render that alternative viable again to be found within the cultural turn? Based on the proposed framework to locate agency in its historical context, the chapter concludes with some critical remarks on the alleged revitalizing effect of a cultural approach for a historical – and interdisciplinary – reasoning on entrepreneurship. Chapter Seven concludes and summarizes the steps taken to turn a descriptive case into an interpretive one.

# Chapter Two  The city-state: A polity with a transactional focus

Abstract:

Genoa, in the 15th and 16th centuries, is the significant context, for it was the place where the two characters found the springboard of their careers in the midst of two critical junctures: the gradual loss of colonies in the Levant by the mid-15th century, and Genoa's integration into the Spanish imperial framework in 1528. At the onset of the considered period, an important process of social change reached its conclusion in the city-state, namely the turning of a merchant class into the dominant class. But worth noting is the fact that such a process materialized in a city-state whereby the city was on the verge of its economic apogee while the state remained a "minimal" one with a weak capacity of enforcing its policies. A state which kept such connotations even after the attempt -from 1528 through1576- to turn it into a regional state such as those of Florence and Venice.[21] Within this backdrop, the chapter recalls

---

21  See, among others, Andrea Zorzi, "Il dominio territoriale di Firenze nei secoli XIV-XV: mediazioni, negoziazioni, pattuizioni," in Francois Foronda (ed.), *Avant le contract social. Le contract politique dans l'Occident médiéval, XIIIe-XVe siecle*, pp. 81–96, Paris, Editions de la Sorbonne, 2011, http://books.openedition.org/psorbonne/ 32809; Matteo Casini, "Fra città-Stato e Stato regionale: riflessioni politiche sullo stato della Repubblica di Venezia in età moderna," *Studi Veneziani*, XLIV, pp. 15–36, 2002; John R. Law, *Venice and the Veneto in the Early Renaissance*, London, Routledge, 2000; Gene Brucker, "Tales of Two Cities: Florence and Venice in the Renaissance Italy," *The American Historical Review*, vol. 88, no. 3, 1983, pp. 599–616; Gherardo Ortalli and Dino Puncuh (eds.), "Genova, Venezia, il Levante nei secoli XII-XIV," *Atti della Società Ligure di Storia Patria*, vol. XLI, (CXV), fasc. 1, 2000, pp.1–17.

the main reasons why a transactional focus kept being well entrenched in the Genoese polity.

**Key words:** merchant capitalism, social dynamics, factional fighting, proto-bourgeoisie, lost colonies, minimal state, feudal persistence.

The establishment of the merchants as a ruling class in late medieval Genoa has been traced back in a detailed archival research in which Quentin Van Doosselaere examines the changes in the coupling between commercial agreements and social dynamics from 1150 through 1425.[22] The first stage of that process is marked by *commenda* contracts in which the partners in long-distant trade are a set of polyvalent actors coming from all corners of society. The only condition of their engagement is the possession of a number of capitals to invest in the venture. However, over the years, long-distance trade tends to become a routine activity solely for a certain

---

For a detailed analysis of the interrelations between legislative and socio-institutional changes, see Rodolfo Savelli, *La Repubblica oligarchica. Legislazione, istituzioni e ceti sociali a Genova nel Cinquecento*, Milano, Giuffré, 1981. On changes in the state administration and the persistent difficulties to govern the mainland, see Giovanni Assereto, *Le metamorfosi della repubblica. Saggi di storia genovese tra il XVI e il XIX secolo*, Genova, Daner, 2000, 77–96. See also, Carlo Bitossi, "L'età di Andrea Doria," pp. 61–78 and, *Idem, La Repubblica di Genova: politica e istituzioni,"* pp. 79–97 both in, Giovanni Assereto and Marco Doria (eds.), *Storia della Liguria*, Bari, Laterza, 2007; Arturo Pacini, *La Genova di Andrea Doria nell'impero di Carlo, V*, Firenze Olschki, 1999.

22  Quentin Van Doosselaere, *Commercial Agreements and Social Dynamics in Medieval Genoa, Cambridge University Press*, 2009, pp. 14–17. The Author examined 11,000 commercial agreements, wills and marriage agreements between 1154 and 1440.

number of merchants increasingly specialized in that kind of pursuit. In fact, between 1340 and 1355, the archival sources show the spread of new contractual agreements that might substitute for the *commenda*: sea loans, change agreements, and promissory notes.[23] Their differences notwithstanding, these contracts represent a crucial turn, for their aim is first and foremost to define the conditions of loan repayments.[24]

Van Doosselaere explains the texture of social relations which transpires from these contractual agreements by specifying the growing complexity of commercial transactions that increasingly require new financial expertise that only the members of commercial and financial elites can master. Thus, at the onset of the 15th century, a significant pattern of social change began to emerge: the financial control of trade turns into a carrier of social privilege. Indeed, the stability of social networks, the high capital base required to enter into a trade partnership, and the frequency of interactions within the same social layer were all elements that added to the stiffening of social structure.[25] The same applies to contracts of maritime insurance, whereby the underwriting is based not so much on market logic as on *insurance pairings* built on expectations of reciprocity. Furthermore, this contractual agreement tends to become something more than an economic tool insofar as its social outcomes make for the consolidation of the oligarchic network.[26]

---

23  However, the first type of agreement already existed in the 12th century under the guise of *bona fide* and *pignum* (pawn) loans. See, Calvin B. Hoover, "The Sea Loan in Genoa in the Twelfth Century," *The Quarterly Journal of Economics*, vol. 40, no. 3, 1926, pp. 495–529, https://doi.org/10.2307/1885175.

24  Van Doosselaere, *Commercial Agreements*, p. 130.

25  Ibid., p. 169.

26  Ibid., pp. 202–207.

Admittedly, in his conclusions, Doosselaere also indicates the plurality of ways through which wealth accumulation took place in late medieval Genoa. As he notes, the process did not involve only the ancient aristocratic families. Several non-nobles and new nobles also enriched themselves with the export of raw materials from the colonies or with military adventures to control the sea trade. Yet, as in other Italian city-states, a different trend emerged as well, that is, the choice of other families to seek government posts as sources of rent and fiscal privileges.[27]

The political and institutional environment in which that kind of merchant capitalism had developed presents an awful scenario of factional fighting punctuated by foreign occupations by France and the Duchy of Milan. This state of affairs may explain the fact that up until the constitutional reform of 1528, the city-state remained an "institutional hybrid" halfway between a Republic and a Signoria that was unable to form into a princedom due to the balance of forces between *cappellazzi* (slouch hats), *popolari*, nobles, Guelphs and Ghibellines. The divisions within the dominant groups, and the endemic conflict with Venice, make the political regime unstable and vulnerable to breakthroughs of external lords and render the city unable to protect the economic interests overseas.[28] Finally, the state keeps being overwhelmed by a huge public debt due to the

---

27  Ibid.

28  Riccardo Musso, "La tirannia dei *cappellazzi*," in Giovanni Assereto e Marco Doria, (eds. ), *Storia della Liguria*, Laterza, 2007, pp. 47–60. *Idem*, "El stato nostro de Zenoa." Aspetti istituzionali della prima dominazione sforzesca su Genova (1464–78), *Serta Antiqua et Medioevalia*, no. 5, 2014, pp. 199–236; Christine Shaw, "Principles and Practice of Civic Government of Fifteenth-Century Genoa," *Renaissance Quarterly*, vol. 58, no. 1, 2005, pp. 45–90.

long-lasting consequences of the Black Death (1346–1353) and the naval defeat with Venice in the battle of Chioggia (1381).[29] Yet, the fact remains that an enduring solution to the debt issue eventually emerges in 1407 under the heading of Bank (House) of Saint George, an institutionalized organization that brought about the debt consolidation thanks to the acquired right to collect the main taxes. However, worth noting is also that the efficient management and the stability of its institutional role turn the *Banco* into a competitor of sort of the Commune. As Riccardo Musso puts it,

> The competition between the two institutions, between the Banco order and the state disorder, becomes a peculiar trait of Genoese history. And the reason also is that the Banco conveys toward its shares the investments not just of aristocrats and wealthy merchants, but also of craftsmen, shop keepers, religious communities, people of the *Riviera*, and foreigners. Thus, the Banco, with its income interests, has really became "all the good and the best of this city."[30]

In the following years, the Genoese state remains almost non-existent, due to the periodical French occupations and the *cappellazzi's* grip on a large part of the *dominio* through local captaincies that had the right to administer justice, appoint the *podestà* (mayor) and collect taxes. De facto, by the mid-15th century, the slouch hats turned into the lords of their districts.

The consequences of this situation for the economy were devastating also because the drubbers were manifold and battle hardened: pirates, street bandits, and local lords. To

---

29  For a chronicle of the revolts and changes in government from 1257 through 1528 see, Steven Epstein, *Genoa and the Genoese, 958-1528*, Chapel Hill, University of Carolina Press, 1996, pp. 325–27.
30  Riccardo Musso, "La tirannia dei cappellazzi," 2007, p. 49.

make matters worse, this was the time of Constantinople's fall (1453), and the beginning of the end for the Genoese colonies in the Levant. It is, therefore, understandable why big merchants decided to deal away from the city, while the rest of them only relied on short-sea transport. Consequently, the contracting out agreement on fiscal policies between the Commune and the Bank of Saint George underwent a drastic change. For more than a century (1446–1562), the Bank was not only entrusted with the fiscal consolidation, but also the full-fledged government of the territories more exposed to risks, both overseas and on the mainland.[31]

The "Men of Saint George" were part of a less exclusivist élite than the Venetian one.[32] They were well-travelled businessmen with administration experience, and well connected in the Mediterranean and Atlantic world. As Jacques Heers points out,

---

31 On the *Banco di San Giorgio*, the classic work is, Heinrich Sieveking: *Studio sulle finanze genovesi nel Medioevo*, in «Associazione Ligure di Storia Patria», Genova, 35 (1905, 1906), vol. I e II. See also, Heers, op. cit., pp. 81–130; Giuseppe Felloni, „A profile of Genoa's Casa di San Giorgio (1407-1805): "A turning Point in the History of Credit, in *Rivista di StoriaEconomica*," 3, 2010, pp. 335–346; Epstein, cit., pp. 260–261 e 277–281. On the last stage in the history of the *Banco*, see Giovanni Assereto "Le vicende del Banco fra la fine del regime aristocratico e l'annessione al Regno di Sardegna," in Giuseppe Felloni (ed.), *La Casa di San Giorgio: il potere del credito*, Genova, Brigati, 2006.

32 However, as Francisco Apellániz shows in his study on the merchants in Alexandria from 1418 to 1420, the role of lower-rank participants as Jews, Greeks, colonial subjects, and foreigners within the exclusive commercial networks of the *Serenissima*, was far from negligible. See, "Venetian Trading Networks in the Medieval Mediterranean," *Journal of Interdisciplinary History*, vol. XLIV, no. 2, 2013, pp. 157–179.

"They do not represent the high aristocracy, but wealthy merchants, financiers, technicians, that is to say, the 'competences', [In such a structure] is the bourgeoisie that rules: a business bourgeoisie that goes from the noble merchant to the notary."[33]

The orientation principle of this managerial class is "order and stability": a principle that can be implemented "only through a firm opposition to every archaic and feudal survivals that may linger on the political organisation of the city."[34] A sketch of such a divide in  the Genoese polity is then required to understand the conduct and context of our two members of that ruling class.[35] However, Medicean Florence reveals itself as a better comparator than Venice to highlight the coupling between socio-economic and institutional dynamics. In that case, the huge amount of public debt was a consequence of the wars against Milan, Lucca and the Papacy from 1424 through 1433. Yet, in Florence, the political crisis would trigger a set of shocks that, contrary to the Genoese ones, eventually led to a centralization of the state under the Signoria of Cosimo de Medici.

Those events have been analyzed by John Padgett and Christopher Ansell in their study on the social networks that underpinned both the Medici's party, and the alliance system

---

33 Jacques Heers, op. cit. p. 93.
34 Ibid., p. 93.
35 Especially for Gioachino da Passano insofar as his birthplace (Levanto) was governed by the Banco in that period and in the same period he was appointed (in 1513) commander of the galleys.

of their rival oligarchs.[36] Besides, they provide a set of data on friendship, kinship and patron-client relations along with evidence on economic partnerships, financial activities and investments in land and real estate. All these archival data depict a relational dynamic that the two authors explain as follows. First, the members of the Florentine oligarchy were connected by dense networks, which did not necessarily fuel collective action, but just individual claims to leadership among individuals of the same social status. On the contrary, the Medici's network was much more centralized, closely-knit and engaging as it included both nobles of a lesser rank, and the "new men" who enriched themselves with the internationalization of trade and finance. Second, Cosimo de Medici emerged as the key actor in the process of institution building, for he proved able to establish new rules that shaped roles, interests, exchanges and patterns of collective action.

As Padgett and Ansell specify, Cosimo is not *The Prince* of Machiavelli: he is a "sphinx" who can pull the strings of the city politics as both judge and boss. He also has the capacity to act in an inexplicit but convincing way with regard to the multiplicity of his interests. He has no official posts, but he can exert a "robust action" because he can avail himself of a forbidding organizational weapon[37]: the "Medici's party" with its peculiar style of social control.[38]

---

36  John Padgett and Christopher Ansell, "Robust Action and the Rise of the Medici, 1400-1434," *American Journal of Sociology*, vol. 98, no. 6, 1993, p. 1262.

37  For a classic study on another organizational weapon, See Philip Selznick, *The Organizational Weapon: A Study of Bolshevik Strategy and Tactics*, New York, McGraw-Hill, 1952.

38  John Padgett e Paul MacLean, "Organizational Invention and Elite Transformation: The Birth of Partnership Systems in Renaissance

In a follow-up research, Padgett and MacLean trace the processes by which kinship, partnership and faction links shape and reproduce economic relations. Specifically, they focus on the rules of action that individuals learn and bring with them through the social and organizational environments in which they will operate over time. A typical example is the rationale of dowry, which shifts from the domain of kinship to that of economic partnership. Another one is the relation master-apprentice that is translated from the domain of guilds to that of international trade, whereby it mingles with that of patrilineal descent. However, the peculiarity of Florence lies in the fact that such kind of organizational changes have an impact on the whole polity economy. In fact, the embedding of economic partnerships within the marriage and patronage networks emerges to be a catalyst of macro-level changes, that is, the rise of a "Republican oligarchy".[39]

Padgett and MacLean indicate that such a trajectory of socio-economic and institutional change differs from those of Genoa and Venice. They assign the specificity of Florence to the strength the action logic of corporatism maintains in that social environment so that even when that rationale is overcome by the power of a new model based on marriage and patron-client links, Florence is oligarchic anew, but in "more relational forms" than elsewhere. It was not the same in Genoa, whereby the legacies of factional fighting were not contrasted enough by the catalyst of change that worked in Florence. The result is the persistence in that polity of a strong "transactional focus" among socio-economic actors that keep interacting according to a short-term rationale.[40]

---

Florence," *American Journal of Sociology*, vol. 111, no. 5, 2006, pp. 1463–1568.
39   Ibid., p. 1473.
40   Ibid., pp. 1545–1546.

Granted, the persistence of a transactional focus in Genoa is a fair point; however, further elaboration is needed on its weaving with forms of relational government that were not lacking in the city. To this aim, a brief account of the contracting out of fiscal policies to the Bank of Saint George may clarify the argument. And the same applies to a less formalized form of hiring out to kinships part of the enforcement burden in the domain of criminal justice in the riotous hinterland a century later.

Specificity of the four centuries' experience of the Bank is the shift from the initial management of fiscal policy and debt consolidation to the political rule over territories on the mainland and overseas. Such a momentous change has its inception when a turn in the Mediterranean economy is to materialize. The Middle Eastern markets must be abandoned along with various colonies in the area (1453–1455), and new economic opportunities must be searched in Europe (Andalusia and Castile). In front of this external shock, the Bank turns into a multitasking organization that is going to manage several matters from the collection of duty taxes to waging wars by enrolling armies, staffing ships, buying provisions, and securing alliances through ambassadors not of the Republic, as of the "House".[41]

---

41  The loss of Genoese colonies in the Aegean and the Black Sea also shows the limits of the Bank of Saint George in its capacity to defend Genoa's interests in the Levant and prevent the corrupt deals in the organization of such endeavour. For instance, contractors that supplied the directors of San Giorgio with mercenaries who either did not exist or who abandoned their duty en route, or quantities of armaments sent to Caffa that went missing from government inventories. (Padraic Rohan, *The Genoese Levantine Colonies at the Birth of Ottoman Imperial Power: A Framework for Enquiry*, master's degree thesis, Graduate School of Social Science, Istanbul Şehir University, p. 87).

In this case of institutionalization and organizational transformation, Steven Epstein quotes Nicolò Machiavelli and his short description of the Bank in *Istorie Fiorentine*, whereby he expressed astonishment regarding the capacity of that organization to take over the government of territories throughout the Genoese *dominio*.[42] Machiavelli also pointed out that the Genoese, despite having repeatedly handed over their state to foreign princes, always kept the Banco firmly in their hands. No state, in Italy and elsewhere, had ever transferred so much power from the institutional structure to a comity of shareholders.[43] He also wondered if the contracting out of government functions to the Banco might not be explained by the fact that such a kind of institutional upheaval was the opposite of what he did advocate for Florence and the other city-states. In other words, the institutionalization of the Bank of Saint George might be conceived of as a "functional alternative"[44] to the building of a "Machiavellian state" as the powerful organizational weapon of the prince.

This point is explained by Matteo Salonia in his account of Genoa's shift from undergoing the "French Fury" of Charles

---

42  Nicolò Machiavelli, *Istorie fiorentine*, Milano, Feltrinelli, 1962.

43  Nowadays, in organization studies, the term institutionalization means getting ethics explicitly into company policy formation, daily decision making and work practices. What was infused into the working of the Bank of Saint George was instead politics, domestic and foreign. On "infusing the organisation with values," a seminal work is, Philip Selznick, *TVA and the Grass Roots. A Study in the Sociology of Formal Organizations*, Berkeley, University of California Press, 1949.

44  For a historical explanation of the role of functional alternatives whereby the typical prerequisites of economic development are lacking, see Alexander Gerschenkron, *Economic Backwardness in Historical Perspective*, Harvard University Press, 1962.

VIII to its embedding into the Spanish imperial framework of Charles V. Salonia stresses that the Banco is to be conceived of as a new organizational form stemming from the institutional mechanism that, from 1363 on, had limited the powers of Genoese political authorities. In essence, such an economic institution was intended to prevent the rising of a *Signoria* and to keep the traditional communal legislation, but it had to do that to the detriment of communal authorities unable to defend the interests of the city overseas and on the mainland.[45] Worse still, by the end of the 15th century, the second stage of the wars of Italy between France and Spain was set in 1498–1516, and the crisis the widening of that conflict brings about appears so deep to call into question the idea itself of city-state.

The overwhelming military power of centralized states shows that a strong army is the true basis of their authority. Yet, after three decades of dire straits, the about-turn of Andrea Doria in 1528 brings Genoa to an institutional solution and a realignment with Spain that rules out the setting up of a *Signoria* aiming at an increased military might and territorial expansion. In the end, Genoa remains "the only Italian polity that stayed true to its late medieval republican beliefs system, in the midst of a geopolitical storm".[46]

The alliance change of 1528 set in motion a process of political bargaining and institution building that would create the basis of the aristocratic republic. Yet the earlier reforms and the "New Laws" (*Leges Novae*) of 1576 did not substantially alter the institutional structure despite some steps ahead in the administrative centralization. The Doge remained in charge for two years, and the prerogatives of the communal government did

---

45  Matteo Salonia, *Genoa's Freedom. Entrepreneurship, Republicanism, and the Spanish Atlantic*, Lanham, Lexington Books, 2017, p. 54.
46  Ibid., p. 105.

not change much so that a widespread judgement on these laws seemed to be "beautiful to see rather than easy to implement".[47] This was apparent, especially for the law which declared the exercise of mechanical arts inconsistent with the noble rank. In the end, the law was emended to ensure the possibility to proceed with current activities "without lapsing from the noble status", but also to become disenfranchised of the political rights connected to that status.[48]

It is worth mentioning here that this body of laws brings about non-negligible changes in the administration of criminal justice. The most significant one is the establishment of a *Rota* made of three foreign jurisconsults empowered to judge in full autonomy all crimes in the city and the *podesterie*. This implies that "no jurisdictional power is left to the *Signoria,* the other magistracies of the city, the Art of Silk or the House of Saint George".[49] However, even in this case, a reverse course began to occur, which ultimately confers the authority on the matter to the Senate and other magistracies in compliance with the traditional local autonomies.

With respect to the Bank of Saint George, at this juncture, it no longer is the government institution it once was. Yet, this does not imply that the geopolitical turn that embedded Genoa into the Spanish imperial framework would trigger patterns of institution-building similar to those undertaken in the regional states with a quite extensive hinterland such as Florence or Venice. All in all, the government of the "Men of Saint George" led Genoa well ahead in its path toward a modern economy.[50]

---

47 Quoted in Savelli, *La repubblica oligarchica"*, p. 233.

48 Ibid., p. 238–239.

49 Ibid., p. 229.

50 See, Avner Greif, *Institutions and the Path to the Modern Economy: Lessons from Medieval Trade*, Cambridge University Press, 2006.

But this did not imply a removal of the hefty feudal survivals still lingering in its *dominio*. Thus, even when the Republic reaches its economic apogee in the "Century of the Genoese" (1528–1627/40),

> "The hinterland of Liguria largely remains a land of feudal lords, castles, desolated areas and jurisdictions of all kind [which] grant safe shelters, sizeable profits and local armies to an aristocracy that often ignores the city and has nothing to do with the Bank of St George whom it perceives as an enemy."[51]

The Genoese *dominio* was not only too narrow to serve as a basis for building a regional state, as the main problem was its socio-economic heterogeneity, which created a gap in the polity between an early modern city and a "Feudal Mountain" in its hinterland. Indeed, what we see here are traces of a re-feudalisation trend that took place to a varying degree in all Italian states between the 16th and the 18th centuries and has been subsumed under the heading of "missed appointment with industrialisation".[52]

---

51  Jacques Heers, *Genova nel '400*, p. 361.

52  Maurice Aymard, "La transizione dal feudalesimo al capitalismo," in Karol Modzelewski et al. (eds.), *Storia d'Italia. Annali I. Dal feudalesimo al capitalismo*, Torino, Einaudi, 1978, pp. 1160–1172. Aymard reassesses the thesis of the "missed appointment with industrialisation", which stems from the incapacity of merchant capitals to influence the organization of production and, more generally, the industrial take off in Italy. On the one hand, the commercial sway in the Mediterranean and north-west Europe lead to a great progress in trading and financial techniques. On the other hand, the widespread practice of granting loans to states and local administrations stimulated a constant increase in the issuance of public securities that, along with land, became the main sources of rent. In short, the Italian mercantile bourgeoisie of

Maurice Aymard traces the causes of the missed opportunity in the early manifestation of new production relationships in agriculture (13th and 14th centuries) which, along with the supremacy of the mercantile cities, brought about a rearrangement of property rights and working methods in a market logic. Yet these traits of the "English model" are somewhat defused by the loss of the economic supremacy of the Italian cities, and by a new political and social equilibrium in which "new aristocracies are going to close ranks to constitute themselves into closed castes".[53] Nonetheless, this interpretation in terms of re-feudalisation leaves room for the capacities of cities to defend

the 16th century would have renounced the pursuing of a socio-economic transformation which was within its reach. Hence, the risk of commerce would be discarded more and more to seek instead sources of rents in the forms of securities, land, real estate, noble titles, and government posts. Aymard contrast this thesis by pointing to the contradictions that emerge at three levels  First, in the urban milieu, new equilibria are going to take shape among social groups, but this goes along with tendencies toward a reshaping of class barriers and the sclerosis of government institutions. Second, the construction of modern regional states, but also the failure of a unification process among these states. Third, the lack of success in the process of internal unification due to the persistence of a rationale of exploitation in the city links with its countryside. In essence, all over the Italian peninsula, one cannot find a modern trait which does not go along with its archaic reversal. However, Aymard surmises that archaisms are not just survivals of the past that weight heavily on the present. Rather, they seem to be a complement more than a contradiction. In a nutshell, he thinks that Italian delays are best explained by the early overcoming of feudalism in the cities that gave to some of them a dominant position in the European economy. Yet, he was more interested in the different development paths of Italian states than in the forms of their internal socioeconomic dualism.

53  Ibid., 1978, p. 1171.

themselves to a certain extent from the feudal legacies through new definitions of social relations and new forms of political participation. Yet, what becomes more difficult, especially for Genoa, is the defence from a much more serious external shock, namely the Islamic expansion in the Western Mediterranean. In fact, what comes to the fore at the onset of the sixteenth century is the "forgotten frontier" between the Habsburg empire and the Ottoman power. As Andrew Hess points out,

> both empires adopted strong defensive postures that, at a time when state power reached new levels, reduced the old zone of mixed cultures to a thin line between well-organized societies. The attendant disappearance of cultural ambivalence along the Ibero-African frontier was the border manifestation of a much larger, unique divergence of Latin Christian and Turko-Muslim civilizations.[54]

Paradoxically, it was such stiffening of the Mediterranean divide in the course of the sixteenth century which virtually eliminated the possibility of cultural experimentation in the very region where innovation in maritime technology drew the world's populations closer together.[55]

Bearing in mind this backdrop, the questions arise: How did the institution building of 1528–1576 allow the aristocratic republic to rein in its Feudal Mountain? How did the two parts

---

54 Andrew, C. Hess, *The Forgotten Frontier. A History of the Sixteenth-Century Forgotten Ibero-African Frontier*, The University of Chicago Press, 2010, p. 207.

55 Ibid. See also, Osvaldo Raggio, *Faide e parentele. Lo stato genovese visto dalla Fontanabuona,* Torino, Einaudi, 1990. A similar case study which provides an interpretive framework of the Ligurian society of that period is, Edoardo Grendi, *Il Cervo e la repubblica. Il modello ligure di antico regime.*

of such a dual polity negotiate their relationships? Who was the subject involved in the negotiations? Many useful insights on these issues, in that historical juncture, can be gleaned by a case study Osvaldo Raggio conducted in the Fontanabuona valley in the Genoese hinterland.[56]

In that period, the Republic was increasingly trying to centralize an administration charged with the management of the private state of a winning aristocracy and an oligarchy in the making. As Raggio specifies, we are not in front of a minor variant of the absolute state nor of a regional state. This was a military and economic component of the Spanish imperial system. However, what must be emphasized is the polycentrism of that system whereby the many nodes would interact among themselves and not solely with the court in Madrid. Within that variety of territorial entities, Naples and Genoa were two central hubs where decisions often took place with scant attention to the directives from the capital city.[57]

The Genoese state was polycentric in its turn with a *dominio* divided between the "owned land" and the "affiliated land."[58] Its local elites were never organized as a government group, but as a set of "principals" in endless competition among themselves

---

56  Raggio, *Faide e parentele*, p. 3.

57  Manuel Herrero Sanchez, *Genova y la Monarquia hispanica (1528–1713)*, Atti della Società Ligure di Storia Patria, vol. LI (CXXV), fasc. 1, 2011; *Idem*, "El modelo republicano en una monarquia de ciudades," in Alain Hugon and Alexandra Merle (eds.), *Soulèvements, Révoltes, Révolutions*, Casa de Velazques, 2017.

58  Ibid. pp.20-24. The problem was that the posts of commissar in the hinterland were almost completely filled by the "poor nobles", the only ones who would accept these unpalatable and badly paid charges. Besides, the enforcement capacities were chronically weak due to a permanent shortage of money to pay the Corsican soldiers assigned to the commissars.

who governed their constituencies through an odd interlocking of formal and informal political mechanisms. However, the commissars sent to administer justice in the hinterland seem to have learned something from their countrymen in other parts of the Spanish imperial framework. As they were not adequately supported by a government with scant capacities to enforce its policies, they were required to find at a local level the resources needed to form an effective administration. To this aim, they needed to transact with local principals and other social actors.[59]

What do the Genoese commissars see in the hinterland? Their reports on the habits of local peoples depict a social world which is archaic in many respects. In the "imperial feuds", local societies are divided into groups, coalitions, and rival factions, but are also connoted by a cultural homogeneity that emerges clearly in their relationships with the city government and the external world. Within this backdrop, Raggio's analysis of the administration of justice in the Fontanabuona may be summarized as follows.

---

59 These operating conditions in the hinterland were markedly similar to those of their counterparts who had to contain smuggling on the see. The only non negligible difference was that better socioconomic conditions on the coast allowed the commissars more room to display an enterprising spirit in their performance. Paolo Calcagno provides some examples in this regard. To make do as they could by recruiting themselves people to patrol the coast or providing local communities with boats to combat smuggling and oblige ship owners to carry out loading and unloading only in the three designated ports of the city-state. To promote the practice of informing by granting the informers one third of the confiscated value, and to propose agreements with local authorities in which lump sum payments freed the involved coastal communities of fiscal obligations. (See, Paolo Calcagno "La lotta al contrabbando," La lotta al contrabbando nel mare Ligustico in età moderna," *Mediterranea*, vol. 7, no. 20, 2010, pp. 484, 485, 495).

The causal link between the short civil war of 1575 and the bursting of banditry in the hinterland is quite evident. Many peasants, recruited by local "captains," took part in that internecine war and, once demobilized, began to gather in armed gangs. However, turning into an outlaw did not amount to being an outcast in the local community.[60] Within his microhistorical framework, Osvaldo Raggio singles out the *parentela* (kinship) as the local counterpart of the city clan, a network that is also the context and language whereby social and political relationships express themselves. In religion, politics and the economy kinship, even if far from being a universal model, is an important organizing force, as it is one of the main reference points that orient individual behaviours and give meaning to their

---

60  This situation may be explained with a reference to the way the defeated clan of Fieschi used to exert its seigniorial power on the eastern coast of Liguria. That power was dependent on the strong links with the local ruling groups, composed of people linked to the noble family by networks of kinship, friendship and patron-client relations. At a lower social level there were family groups of merchants and craftsmen among whom *podestas* and lieutenants of various sort were chosen. Finally, the many peasant kinships that could be mobilized for factional struggles if required. As Riccardo Musso explains, the popularity of the Fieschi family was due to a shrewd combination of authoritarianism and paternalism "capable to strongly chastise those who did not comply with their orders (possibly by burning their houses or killing their livestock). However, it was also due to their readiness to offer protection on judicial matters, to help financially those asking for a subsidy or to pay the tax on land properties (*avaria*) to those affiliated with the Guelph faction." (Riccardo Musso, "Le fazioni nel medio Levante ligure tra XV e XVI secolo," in Giuliana Algeri and Valeria Polonio (eds.), *L'Oratorio dei disciplinanti di Moneglia. Testimonianza di fede e di arte nella storia di una comunità*, Atti del Convegno, Moneglia, 10–11 ottobre 2008.

relationships.[61] Parental solidarity was then to be transposed into the criminal legislation of the Genoese state in the form of collective responsibility for the action of those kin who turned into street bandits. This applies to the lesser crimes dealt with "pacification contracts" whereby kinships engage themselves in the expulsion of the outlaws from the territory that the city government is not able to enforce. Thus, despite attempts to centralize the administration, several autonomies were required to be granted to local communities.

To conclude, the transactional focus was well entrenched in Renaissance Genoa, and often mingled with forms of relational governance based on mutual trust and cooperation. Such governance was not highly efficient; however, it was somewhat capable of maintaining the integrity of the city-state and a certain degree of social consensus so that someone felt obliged to write, "...*sotto il felice e dolce dominio della Serenissima Repubblica*".[62]

---

61  Raggio, *Faide e parentele*, p. 9.

62  "Under the blessed and sweet dominion of the *Serenissima Repubblica*." See, Giovanni Assereto and Giuseppe Bongiovanni, *Sotto il felice e dolce dominio della Serenissma Repubblica. L'acquisto di Finale da parte di Genova e la distinta relazione di Filippo Cattaneo De Marini*, Savona, Daner, 2003. On the governance in the borderlands of the city-state see, Giovanni Assereto, *Le metamorfosi della repubblica. Saggi di storia genovese tra il XVI e XIX secolo*, Daner, 1999; Andrea Zanini, "Strategie politiche ed economia feudale ai confini della Repubblica di Genova (secoli XVI-XVIII)," *Atti della Società ligure di storia patria*, XLV–CXIX, 2005.

# Chapter Three    Bartolomeo da Framura: Manager on the alum fields

**Abstract:**
The initial setting of the transprofessional career of Bartolomeo was Framura – the village in which he was born – and Genoa soon after, whereby he will begin to display business acumen and an ability to build up his political clout. This chapter describes the main steps of this career with a focus on the management of the Pope's alum quarries after the loss of Genoese colonies and mines in the Levant.

**Key words:** transprofessional career, purchase of offices, procurement contracts, Church's administration, new crusades

## 3.1. Merchant within a trading and ecclesiastical network

Bartolomeo, at the beginning of his career in Genoa, is depicted by Jacques Heers in this brief portrait:

> In Genoa, Bartolomeo da Framura is an immigrant and sure enough he brings the name of his native village. His patrimony is that of a countryman […]. Granted, his wealth is not necessarily sizeable, nonetheless he possesses a house with a porch in the main square, and another one in the same village. He is a landowner, and he keeps buying land. He sells wine and also fustians and canvasses he brings with him. He lends money. In his area he may be regarded as an important

character, a man who made one's fortune, piles up money and claims to be saluted as *nobilis vir*.[63]

At the onset of the 15th century, Bartolomeo is a prominent personality among his fellow countrymen that settled in Genoa as silversmiths, merchants and craftsmen. In 1406 his father, a wealthy furrier, designates him as a sole heir while Bartolomeo is somewhere in the Mediterranean to take care of his affairs along those of the noblemen Eliano Spinola.[64]

The first archival evidence of Bartolomeo's activities dates from 1416 when he becomes vice-municipal chancellor, but detailed accounts of his activities do emerge only forty years later. At that juncture he is an asset administrator for several of his countrymen, the most important of whom is the noble Pellegro de Mondello who proves quite useful for the widening of Bartolomeo's business which is going to include the purchase of procurement for the tax collection in Sardinia. However, sea trade remains his main activity which consists almost exclusively of importing cheese from the island. In the meantime, the *podesteria* of Framura remains the base for his trade of grains.

In 1458, while civil war and the plague ravage Genoa, Bartolomeo and some of his important friends take refuge in Framura until 1460, the year in which his links with patricians and exponents of the pontifical curia are going to consolidate. Links that bring about excellent results. In fact, Eliano Spinola makes a thousand golden ducats mortgage loan to Bartolomeo to buy the *scriptoria apostolica*. The next year also comes the

---

63  Heers, op. cit., p. 329.

64  The Spinola's business network also included Giovanni da Pontremoli who was not only a merchant engaged in import-export activities, but a tax collector for the Bank of Saint George (see, Matteo Salonia, *Genoa's Freedom*, pp. 35–61).

clerical status for Bartolomeo's twelve year's son, granted by Pius II thanks to the intercession of the nobleman Prospero Adorno.[65] The Genoese Curia in its turn mandate that the *vir egregius, nuncius et scriptor apostolicus* be not prosecuted for possible debts and obligations, neither by the Genoese magistracies nor by private citizens. The Roman Curia is instead going to favour the expansion of his economic activities with the joint participation in the use of alum quarries of Tolfa, near Civitavecchia.[66] This happens within the backdrop of a critical

---

65  Lercari, op. cit., 2017, p. 356. The buying and selling of offices in the papal court began around mid-15th century and was managed by the *Uffici Venali* that established the prices according to the prestige and privileges stemming from the assigned post. If buyers did not possess all the amount due, they could ask for credit to one or more individuals in exchange for a quota of the rents coming from the assignment. For an example of how the dealing was negotiated between the Venal offices, the buyers and the lenders see, Anna Esposito, "La pratica delle compagnie d'uffici alla corte di Roma tra fine '400 e inizio '500," in Jamme, Armand and Olivier Poncet, *Offices, écrits et papauté (XIIIe-XVIIe siècle)*, Publication de l'Ecole française de Rome, 2007, pp. 497–515. For a framing of the buying and selling of positions within the procurement system of the papal court see, Francesco Guidi Bruscoli, "Mercanti-banchieri e appalti pontifici nella prima metà del Cinquecento," in *Idem*, pp. 517–532.

66  On Bartolomeo's activities in Genoa and the Papal court see, Andrea Lercari, "Una comunità ligure di antico regime: personaggi e famiglie framuresi tra XV e XVIII secolo, " pp. 336–361 in A. Lercari (ed.), *Framura. Un'antica terra ligure fra il mare e i monti*, Genova, AGF 2017. For a general view of political and military dynamics of the alum trade when Bartolomeo was one of the managers in Tolfa see, Jean Delumeau, *L'alun de Rome. XV-XIXe siècle*, S.E.V.P.E.N. 1962; Benjamin Weber, "Lutter contre le Turcs: Les formes nouvelles de la croisade pontificale au XVe siecle (l'alun de Tolfa)," *Collection de l'Ecole française de Rome*, no. 42, 2013, pp. 315–324; Ivana Ait, "Dal governo signorile al governo mercantile: i monti della Tolfa

juncture in the Genoese history which is worth recounting, even if in broad terms.

The monopolist management of alum field in the Levant by consortia run by Genoese aristocratic families begins in the second half of the 13th century and goes on for more than two centuries fuelling a great volume of trade, especially with England and the Flanders. This is a topic widely dealt with in the historiography of Genoa.[67] In what follows, I just draw an outline of what

---

e le 'lumere' del papa," in *Mélanges de l'Ecole française de Rome-Moyen Age*, 126-1, 2014, pp. 1–59.

67  See, among others, Enrico Basso, "Prima di Tolfa: i mercanti genovesi e l'allume orientale," *Melanges de l'Ecole française de Rome-Moyen Age. 126-1, 2014; Idem, Insediamenti e commercio nel Mediterraneo bassomedievale: i mercanti genovesi dal Mar Nero all'Atlantico*, Torino, Marcovalerio, 2008; Claude Cahen, "L'alun avant Phocêe," *Revue d'Histoire économique et sociale*, vol. 41, no. 4, 1963, pp. 433–447; Richard Kressel, *The administration of Caffa under the Uffizio di San Giorgio*, Madison, University of Wisconsin, 1966; Roberto Lopez, *Storia delle colonie genovesi nel Mediterraneo*, Bologna, Marietti, 1996 [1938]; Giangiacomo Musso, "Il tramonto di Caffa genovese," in *Miscellanea di storia ligure in memoria di Giorgio Falco*, pp. 311–339, Fonti e Studi, 1966; Geo Pistarino, "The Genoese in Pera – Turkish Galata," *Mediterranean Historical Review*, vol. 1, no. 1, 1986, pp. 63–85; Pietro Saraceno, "L'amministrazione delle colonie genovesi nell'area del Mar Nero dal 1261 al 1453," *Rivista di storia del diritto italiano* 42/43, 1969, pp. 177–226; Daniel Goffman, *The Ottoman Empire and Early Modern Europe*, Cambridge University Press, 2004; Louis Mitler, "The Genoese in Galata: 1453-1682," *International Journal of Middle East Studies*, vol. 10, no. 1, 1979, pp. 71–91; Giustina Olgiati, "The Genoese Colonies in Front of the Turkish Advance (1453-1475)," *Tarih Araṛṣtirmalari Dergisi*, vol. 15, no. 26, 1991, pp. 381–389, https://dergipark.org.tr; Jacques Heers, *Genova nel 400*, pp. 279–82; Ievgen Alexandrovitch Khvalkov, *The Colonies of Genoa in the Black Sea Region: Evolution and Transformation,*

happened during the crumbling of colonial administrations in various regions of the Levant due to the Turkish conquest. In doing this, I draw mainly on Enrico Basso's pivotal account of both the strategic management of consortia and the geopolitics of the alum import from the Levant until it was kept viable.[68]

The first ones who tried to go ahead with trade monopoly were Benedetto and Manuele Zaccaria who did follow a scheme in continuity with that practised before the conquest of Chios and Focea by the Turks in 1453.[69] The strategy the two brothers are going to implement stems from a simple fact: the payment of a monetary tribute to the Ottoman power turns out to be sustainable due to the high demand for alum in Western markets. In that period, commercial prospects remained positive, even under the new political order, due not just to the monetary tribute paid by the Genoese, and the relative benevolence of Sultan Mehmed II. If anything, the problem for the stakeholders of alum trade was due more to the general political situation and the relationships of Genoa with the western powers.[70]

---

Degree Thesis, European University Institute, Florence, Department of History and Civilization, 2015.

68  Enrico Basso, "Prima di Tolfa," p. 27.

69  The bigger informal cartel that existed before the Ottoman advance began to operate in 1448 and got formally established in 1449. It gathered all the most important contractors of the alum fields under the guidance of Francesco Draperio, and exported the impressive amount of 23,824 tons of material in six years. (See, Enrico Basso, "Prima di Tolfa," p. 45).

70  An example was the serious litigation opened up in 1458 between the Genoese and the British due to repeated acts of piracy by members of the Gattiluso house to the detriment of English trade navigation in the Mediterranean. The dispute was closed in 1466 by a commercial deal managed by the Bank of Saint George who placed a batch of alum on the Flemish market to draw enough money to pay

The leading actor of the last attempt to revive the alum extraction and trade was instead Paride Giustiniani who, between 1456 and 1459, would display a two-pronged strategy: first, to raise alum extraction in Mytilene to the greater extent to offset the lack of supplies from Anatolia; second, to start discreet negotiations with the Sultan in order to be awarded the contract of Focea's fields along with the possibility to restart local production of alum. This would have allowed the new company to pile up great stocks of material not in Chios as was the case before, but in places in the West less exposed to the Turkish threat.[71] Moreover, Mehmed II did not dismiss the idea of sharing the earnings from the selling of alum, an attitude that prompted the drafting of an official proposal to be sent to him by the Genoese for trade cooperation. The proposal was discussed by the *Gran Consiglio* in Genoa but in the end not implemented, perhaps due to the fear of running into the Pope's anger, or to avoid thwarting the shipping of alum to the West by Genoese traders.[72] Thus the final date for the export of alum to Atlantic

6,000 pounds to the English Crown and the damaged ship owners. (See Enrico Basso, "La presenza genovese in Inghilterra e le relazioni commerciali anglo-genovesi nella seconda metà del XV secolo," in Marcella Arca Petrucci and Simonetta Conti (eds.), *Giovanni Caboto e le vie dell'Atlantico Settentrionale*, Roma, CISGE, 1999, pp. 17–39.

71  Enrico Basso, Prima di Tolfa, p. 66; See also Pistarino, "The Genoese in Pera," and Olgiati, "The Genoese Colonies in Front of the Turkish Advance," pp. 386–390.

72  Jean Delumeau, *L'alun de Rome, XVe-XIXe siecle*, S.E.V.P.E.N. 1990, pp. 82–90. In a "New World" that was rising from the wars and the Reform, collaborating with the English king -who turned into an enemy of the Pope and the Habsburg- was unthinkable. Thus the noble merchants of Genoese families in the end come to realize that the time was ripe to redirect their affairs toward the Iberian markets(Basso, "Prima di Tolfa," p. 66). The Pope referred to here

Europe will be around 1566 when the fall of Chios marks the definitive loss of a key piece which had long been linking all the branches of alum trade from the Aegean, toward the West.

As Enrico Basso suggests, if we were to seek the ideal type of a Genoese merchant in the golden age of the Ligurian commerce, we would find it in a portrait Roberto Lopez made of Benedetto Zaccaria, merchant and admiral in the 13th century Genoa.[73] Indeed, that great entrepreneur was able to impose a monopoly on the most important Eastern alum fields, and thus turned into a role model of sort for those who have followed in the running and trading of that strategic resource. Bartolomeo da Framura was one of them.

---

was Enea Silvio Piccolomini, pope Pius II (1458–64), the one who contracted-out the running of alum fields to Bartolomeo da Framura and his two partners. Pius II was a pope of his time, nepotist and patronizing. But he was patron of the arts as well insofar as he wanted to turn his native town –Pienza- into a model of "humanist city". Before acquiring the ecclesiastic status, he was a scholar and ambassador of great stature who contributed to the solidity of bonds between the Roman Curia and the Court of Vienna. During his papacy he went ahead with his conciliatory policy toward the German Court. In the personality of this pope one may also find a medieval mysticism of sort whose main expression was a kind of "Crusader ardour" that caused him to rack his brain about the way to counteract the Turks, enemies of Christianity and the Roman civilization. Pius II will in the end engage in this mission the riches yielded by the Tolfa alum fields. And he dies in Ancona in the lead-up of an unrealistic 'crusade' which never started due to the lack of involvement from Christian princes. (Franco Cardini, Pio II, in *Enciclopedia Europea*, vol. VIII, Garzanti, 1979, pp. 965–66).

73 See Roberto Lopez, *Benedetto Zaccaria: ammiraglio e mercante nella Genova del Duecento*, Genova, Frilli, 2004 [1933].

## 3.2. Contractor and trader in the Papal quarries (1460–1466)

The alum fields of Tolfa are believed to have been discovered between 1460 and 1462 – at the onset of the Papacy of Pius II – by Giovanni de Castro, Bartolomeo da Framura and Carlo Gaetani. In the first procurement contract, Bartolomeo is depicted as *Genoese citizen, our writer and relative.* Genoese as well are the companies that will trade the alum of Tolfa as they used to do with their consortia in the Levantine colonies.

When Bartolomeo reaches Rome he gets embedded in a context in which the Genoese presence within both the Pontifical state structure, and the trade and financial activities begins to consolidate, especially under the Papacy of Sixtus IV and Innocent VIII, both Genoese.[74] This is the environment in which the newly discovered alum fields are going to acquire strategic importance for a Papacy that aims to acquire the monopoly of extraction and trade. And this implies a monopoly for the Genoese companies as well. Yet this aim is not easy to implement because of the need to take into account the disputes and compromises between Genoese and Tuscan contractors. That is why the Genoese get for them the sole right of transport and selling of alum between Genoa and London.[75]

The first procurement contract is signed in 1462, and includes a provision that reminds how feudalism is still lingering in the

---

74  Jan Delumeau, *Vie economique et social de Rome dans la seconde moitié du XVIe siècle*, Paris, De Boccard, 1959.

75  Diego Pizzorno, *Genova e Roma fra Cinque e Seicento. Gruppi di potere, rapporti diplomatici, strategie internazionali*, Modena, Mucchi Editore, 2018, pp. 23–29; Franceso Guidi Bruscoli, Mercanti-banchieri e appalti pontifici nella prima metà del Cinquecento in, *Offices, écrits et papauté (XIIIe XVIIe siècles)*, Publications de l'Ecole française de Rome, 2007, pp. 517–532.

local environment, for it entitles the three contractors to carry with them defensive and offensive weapons along with an armed escort. That was because armed gangs of feudal lords or street bandits could threaten the alum business. The next contract of 1466 is undertaken by the Medici family until 1478, along with other Genoese merchants mostly related to the previous ones. This contract sanctions the entry of the Medici family into the alum company in place of Bartolomeo da Framura, deceased the same year. The agreement of 1471 is signed under the Papacy of Paul II – successor of Pius II – who is worried about the competition of the alum mines in the Tuscan town of Volterra and seeks not to lose the Medici as customers. Four years later, the Pazzi take the place of Medici, but just up to 1478 when their plot in Florence against the Medici fails. In the following years until 1491, there is an alternation in management between the Medici and Genoese families with a volume extracted of around 1,200 tons per year.[76]

Worth mentioning in the management of Tolfa mines is the financial supervision of the *Camera Apostolica* which defines (in the second contract of 1465) the following conditions for a new engagement of Papacy in the alum company. First, to establish in advance, for the nine successive years, the quota of the volume extracted to be devolved to the Church's financial administration. Second, to engage this general commission to purchase the product at a price defined by the contract. Third, to divide equally the profits among the three contractors by the expiry date. Also well detailed are the clauses on the expenses to maintain the efficiency of the extraction process in a plant quite similar to a company town. The three partners had to buy the machinery themselves and had the obligation to maintain and

---

76  Duleaumeau, "L'alun de Rome," p. 89.

renovate them. They also had to build lodgings for the miners, and to manage hiring and the payment of salaries.[77]

The three contractors could also act as sole traders, and it is in this light that we can see their search for investment capital due to the need to delegate the commercial function to merchant-bankers companies with many branches and agencies. Thus Bartolomeo and Carlo Caetani assigned their trade to Piero de Medici, so much so that the Medici family had gotten back the depository of the Apostolic Chamber.[78]

As for the period in which the exploitation of Tolfa mines begins, two crucial issues must be recalled. First, the funding of the struggle against the Turks makes the monopoly of alum trade necessary. However, the theoretical simplicity of such statement (repeated in various Papal bulls) goes along with many difficulties of putting it into practice during the first decade of mining activity. Benjamin Weber traces back such difficulties through an examination of archival evidences on the *Camera Sancte Cruciate* (Chamber for the Holy Crusade) created to finance the war against the Ottoman along with the comments

---

77  Ait, "Dal governo signorile al governo mercantile," pp. 22–23. On the *Camera Apostolica* and the ways in which it combined charitable, productive and financial purposes see, Donatella Strangio, "Public Debt in the Papal States, Sixteenth to Eighteenth Century," *Journal of Interdisciplinary History*, vol. 43, no. 4, 2013, pp. 511–537.

78  The Medici themselves owned alum mines in Tuscany (beside that of Volterra) which were directed by people who had professional paths quite similar to that of Bartolomeo da Framura and his two partners. See Donata Degrassi, "L'impresa mineraria nel tardo Medioevo: competenze, tecniche, organizzazione, mobilità geografica e sociale," pp. 25–49 in, Lorenzo Tanzini and Sergio Tognetti, *La mobilità sociale nel Medioevo italiano. Competenze, conoscenze e saperi tra professioni e ruoli sociali* (secc. XII-XV), Roma, Viella, 2016.

and the biography of Pius II. These sources show that Giovanni de Castro present the discovery of the alum fields in Tolfa to the Pope in the following terms: "Now you can get ready for the war against the Turks. This mine will give you the strength and money necessary for the war and take them away from the Turks."[79] Yet, the periodical reports on the extraction activity by the two partners to the Apostolic Chamber do not contain any reference to the war against the Ottomans. Thus Weber surmises, based on some evidence on the prices of alum, that the real intention of Pius II was to counteract the enduring monopoly of Genoese traders by the sole company that Francesco Draperio established in 1449. A field outside that monopoly was then a strategic resource to the Pope, and as such it required something more than a mere profit-sharing by the pontifical administration. Hence, if the first agreement reserved to the Chamber a 15 % share of profits, in the new one the Chamber acts as the sole buyer and seller of the extracted alum. And the selling prices are two to five times higher than those of the purchase.[80]

Pius II's search for higher incomes from the alum trade is related to the crusade he intends to organize, but this is much more a rhetorical exercise than a concrete project. In other words, the periodical papal bulls simply prohibited the import of alum from Ottoman territories, but not from the Aragonese, Neapolitan or Castilian ones. Even if, in 1464, this Pope actually tries to set sail from Ancona (whereby he dies) for the crusade he yearned for. Only the Venetians responded to his plea and provided just a few galleys.[81]

---

79  Benjamin Weber, "Lutter contre le Turcs: les formes nouvelles de la croisade pontificale au XVe siècle," *Collection de l'Ecole française de Rome*, no. 472, 2013.

80  Ibid., pp. 7–11.

81  Ibid., p. 19.

Under the next papacy of Paul II (1464–1471) the Chamber for the Holy Crusade keeps being administered by a committee of cardinals that deals both the alum issue and that of the Ottoman advance in Europe. Now the depositary of the Chamber is again the Medici bank which had previously performed the same task for the Apostolic Chamber. However, at least till the end of 1466, the Medici's grip on the mines remains quite loose. Accountability is still the task of the three partners who keep in practice the role of depositaries.

As for the geopolitical scenario in which these events are going to take place, Benjamin Weber makes this synthesis:

> Alum could have remained a purely technical and economic issue, prerogative of the Apostolic Chamber. In order to get higher benefits and impose its monopoly, the Papacy associated the issue to the war against the Turks [However] at an historical juncture in which the Papal power was increasingly contested (...) to impose the Christians to buy the Tolfa alum was surely a means that accrued to the economic power of Papacy. But it was even more a display of the pontifical dominion, that is something that was deemed unacceptable by Christian princes engaged in remarking upon their national sovereignty. [82]

Weber's conclusion then is that the root causes of the Papal failure were to be searched not much on the quantity, quality and prices of alum rocks as in these implications not only political, but symbolic as well.

This is the scenario in which the case of Bartolomeo da Framura was framed. A scenario which marks the initial stiffening of a Mediterranean divide between Christendom and the Muslim word which impinges on his business strategies as it does for the whole merchant class in Genoa and the Levant.

---

82  Ibid., p. 31.

However, the typicality of this form of entrepreneurial agency needs to be also highlighted with reference to the cases of two of his countrymen: Agostino Grancelli, and Giovanni da Pontremoli. Agostino, born as Bartolomeo in Framura, may be considered the most current model of Ligurian merchant between the sixteen and the seventeenth century. The business he ran allowed him to pile up wealth, but mostly in the same manner, that is, by shipping cargoes of paper between Genoa and Seville. He was a business partner of the noblemen Bartolomeo Donghi, who owned the paper mills in Genoa and was kindred with the Da Passano family, but his agency relationships remained those of a ship owner and trader to the west Mediterranean.[83]

A better comparative reference for Bartolomeo's entrepreneurial action is the transprofessional career of an upwardly mobile socio-economic actor in Medicean Florence. The character was Tommaso Marinai, a son of an itinerant notary who succeeded, thanks to his know-how, in becoming a very young director of a mining enterprise. But he also became a financing partner in it thanks to his "know who", that is, his consociation with characters in the higher echelons of Florentine polity economy. Thus he became able to invest in real estate in an area nearing his mine and, with his reputation and uncommon knowledge, he made his way up to the summits of power and turned into the referent of Lorenzo de Medici in mining matters.[84]

In his analysis of the correspondence between Giovanni da Pontremoli and his representatives, Matteo Salonia depicts another case of a businessman who expanded his capital and made investments not just to increase productivity ad speed up transport,

---

83  See, Bruno Grancelli, *Nobili, mercanti e navigatori framuresi*, Carrara, Impressum Edizioni, 2019, pp. 120–131.

84  Donata Degrassi, "L'impresa mineraria nel medioevo." pp. 25–50.

but to gather data on the merchandises present in various markets and the fluctuation of prices. Salonia sees the life of this merchant as a typical application of the Genoese economic culture. In fact, Giovanni (the same as Bartolomeo) was a tax collector, an activity that he likely saw as a way to pile up enough money to start up his own import-export business and get embedded into the Genoese merchant community.[85] A second aspect of the typicality of this form of entrepreneurial agency is that the displacement of investments and activities from the Levant to the Ibero-Africa frontier was decided not by following a communal policy, but by taking advantage of previous activities along that frontier.[86]

In his contextualization of the story of Giovanni da Pontremoli, Salonia stresses the multiformity of activities of the Genoese as individuals driven by a mercantile mentality and a proto-capitalist ideology. But he also points to their awareness of "negative pressures [such as] the internal and external predatory powers threatening their entrepreneurship and jeopardizing a stable prosperity in the cosmopolitan networks they had built." In short, What such a political culture brought about in the Genoese polity was a widespread desire to protect the rule of law, to limit the power of the Doge to create a financial self-government through the Bank of Saint George. According to Salonia, such a kind of entrepreneurial mindset and the intercontinental business it brought about is a clear example of market expansion, private economic calculation and adaptability over time.[87] But the story of Bartolomeo da Framura, and even more of Gioachino da Passano, show that one cannot skip over the patterns of social advancement and the possible changes in the forms of agency and its embeddedness in the shifting contexts whereby adaptability is going to take shape.

---

85  Matteo Salonia, *Genoa's Freedom,* Lexington Books, 2017, p. 36.
86  Ibid., p. 44.
87  Ibid., p. 55.

# Chapter Four  Gioachino da Passano: Trusted men of King Francis I

**Abstract:**

Gioachino da Passano (Levanto 1465–Padua 1551) belonged to a noble family settled in various areas of the Genoese *dominio* which held important privileges, but was not in a central position within the Genoese political power.[88] Da Passano was nearly the same age as admiral Andrea Doria, and shared with him part of his career path which was military and political, but began with the trading of grains and financial activities. As Guillome Alonge notes, the apex of this transprofessional and transnational career is to be framed within a history still mostly to be written relating the agents of King Francis I of Valois "wandering Europe and the Mediterranean on the trail of new allies, even among infidels and heretics, with the aim to counteract the progression of the Habsburg power."[89] This chapter presents some stylized facts on the agency relationships of one of these characters in Genoa and France.

**Key words:** multiplicity of careers, wars of Italy, political entrepreneurship, geopolitical strategist.

---

88　Andrea Lercari, "Tra grande patriziato e notabilato locale: i da Passano nella Repubblica di Genova," *Giornale Storico della Lunigiana e del Territorio Lucense*, anni LX-LXII, pp. 259–346.

89　Guillome Alonge, "Evangelismo e ortodossia nella diplomazia Franco-Turca di Francesco I," *Melanges de l'Ecole française de Rome*, 129-2, 2017, p. 1.

## 4.1. Merchant and commander of the galleys

At the onset of 1500, Gioachino da Passano begins positioning himself within the Fregoso faction which includes both Andrea Doria and the family of Pope Julius II (1503–1513) who appoints him the first of his many political assignments. Thus, in 1512 he is by the Duke of Urbino to settle some disputes he had with his uncle the pope after he had appointed the nephew "General of the Church's galleys" and conferred him the *Signoria* of Pesaro.

The next year, Ottaviano Fregoso succeeds in removing the pro-French governor of Genoa and takes for himself the Dogeship with the Spanish support. The new regime hurries to rebuild the fleet and appoints Gioachino da Passano "Commander of the galleys."[90] That was during the third War of Italy (1508–1516) between France and Spain. In that period, Gioachino takes part in some clashes in Genoa against the French who retreats from the city in 1514. And the same year he leaves the city to go to the Papal court of Leo X (1513–1521). There he goes to plead the concession of the cardinal's purple to Innocenzo Cybo, nephew

---

90  As Steven Epstein notes, in the five preceding centuries, there had never been a situation in which the Muslim naval power was so strong and the Genoese fleet so weak. Yet, Genoa gets dragged into the many French wars. As an example, Eptein refer to the involvement into the League of Cambrai (1508) created by the emperor Maximiliam of Habsburg, Luis XII, Pope Julius II and Ferdinand of Aragon to contain the expansionism of Venice. (See, Steven Epstein, *Genoa and the Genoese, 958-1528*, The University of Carolina Press, 1996). Another sign of the persistent weakness of the fleet were the continuous forays of the Saracens pirates on the Ligurian coast. See, for instance, Giorgio Casanova, "Framura e il mare: una vocazione millenaria tra pescatori, naviganti e corsari," in Andrea Lercari (ed.), *Framura: un'antica terra ligure fra il mare e i monti"*, pp. 857–926.

of the former Pope Innocent VIII (1484–1492). Even Leo X appoints him General of the Church's galleys, an office he cannot occupy, for he falls prisoner of the Turks for several months. When he is set free, the doge Fregoso appoints him commander of the troops of the Republic.[91]

In the meantime in France Luis XII was succeeded (in 1515) by Francis I, son of Charles of Valois and Louise of Savoy. And Genoa does what it already did before; that is, it places itself under the sovereignty of the French king. In that same year a battle breaks out in Marignano (Melegnano) for the control of the Duchy of Milan whereby the main contenders are France and Switzerland. Francis I, the winner, will govern the Duchy until 1521. Genoa did play a minor role in that war with the limited aim to reconquer some territories in its hinterland. Yet, this scenario marks a turning point in the career of Gioachino da Passano who is sent to France to inform the king on the military operations Genoa was involved in.

The ambassador also takes part in the post-war negotiations to redefine the northern borders of the city-state. At that point in time the French king holds the Genoese envoy back in his court as an advisor and senior steward in the house of his mother. Then, Francis I appoints da Passano ambassador by the emperor Charles V, something that allows him to become the referent both for Genoese merchants in the Flanders under the Spanish rule, and the Genoese citizens that had private matters to settle with French authorities. All these functions must have been admirably performed given that the Commune of Genoa nominates the ambassador *sindico, nunzio et oratore* to the French court.[92] He was also praised in France for his ability to

---

91 Andrea Lercari, *Tra grande patriziato e notabilato locale*, vol. 1, p. 186–187.

92 Ibid., p. 264–265.

raise funds and negotiate peace treatises, princely marriages and the liberation of prestigious hostages.[93]

Then comes the next of Italian wars (1521–1526) which was the worst of all for it quickly brings to the sack of Genoa (1522) that foreshadows that of Rome in 1527. The origin of all that lies in the French attempt to reconquer Milan which pushes Charles V (king of Spain, Naples and Sicily) to send an army of Spaniards, Landsknechts, Italians and Genoese exiled against Genoa. The result of the short siege was the sack and the state collapse which leads to the expulsion of Fregoso from the Dogeship and his replacement by Antoniotto Adorno.

At that juncture, Gioachino da Passano is in France whereby he purchases the *Seigneurie* of Vaux. There his negotiation skill will be hard tested when he is entrusted by the Council of Regency with the task of dealing with the liberation of Francis I, defeated and captured in the battle of Pavia (1525) by Charles V. The ransom is paid and the French king is liberated after a year with the promise to give up his pretences on Italy. But soon enough Francis I resumes the initiative to weaken the emperor. To this aim, ambassador da Passano is sent to England to obtain from Henry VIII the agreement for a peace treaty with France. This mission is also successful so that the English king appoints da Passano procurator for the territories to be given back to the French queen, the widow of Louis XII.

Da Passano will have one more time an important role in the negotiation for the shaping of the anti-Spanish League of Cognac between England, France, the Papacy, Venice and Milan. During the fifth Italian war (1526–1530), the ambassador turns again into a man of arms as commissar and lieutenant of the French army that should have conquered Naples. Such a task was

---

93  Associazione Dimore Storiche Italiane, (Section Ligure, Actes du congrès 2011), *Mémoires de Luise de Savoie, 1476-1531* (BNF).

indeed performed along with some other diplomatic mediations all along the Italian peninsula.[94] However, these diplomatic successes are framed in a scenario in which France is doomed because it has been invaded by England, and Francis I is no longer in condition to recover the lost territories in Northern and Southern Italy. And it is such a backdrop that explains the political and institutional turn which begins in 1528 when Andrea Doria takes over Genoa with his squadron of galleys.[95]

## 4.2. Geopolitical strategist on the French side

The Doria's turn takes place at the onset with the French backing that however turns into an alliance with Spain in a matter of months. Even after Doria shifted sides, the ambassador keeps his activity at the service of the French king which includes the mediation between the rival republics of Venice and Genoa. Gioachino ends his military and diplomatic service in 1530–1534 again as ambassador to England to revise the extant agreements between that country and France. He is also been sent to Venice and appointed general superintended for the affairs of Francis I in Italy.[96]

The point worth emphasizing here is that the events in these five years at the French court are highly significant to deepen our

---

94  Lercari, "Tra grande patriziato e notabilato," p. 267.

95  On the political and institutional outcomes of the Doria's turn, see, Arturo Pacini, *La Genova di Andrea Doria nell'impero di Carlo V*, Firenze, Olschki, 1999 and, *I presupposti politici del secolo dei genovesi: la riforma del 1528*, SLSP, 1990; Carlo Bitossi, "L'età di Andrea Doria," in Giovanni Assereto and Marco Doria (eds.), *Storia della Liguria*, pp. 61–78, 2007, Bari, Laterza; Rodolfo Savelli, *La repubblica oligarchica. Legislazione, istituzioni e ceti a Genova nel Cinquecento*, Milano, Giuffré, 1981.

96  Ibid., p. 275.

knowledge of the activities of this character and more generally, to grasp the role of the resident ambassador in the genealogy of the national state that was going to establish itself in Europe. Indeed, in the lead up to the Century of the Genoese we may notice two main forms of entrepreneurial agency on both sides of the geopolitical space disputed by France and Spain. The first country mostly attracts skilful political actors who make their career in court and the state administration while the second does the same, but also integrate lots of Genoese in its economic and military structures through a widespread system of contracting out (*asientos*). Gioachino da Passano falls into the first category of upwardly mobile actors on the French side while Andrea Doria gets involved in the polity economy of the Spanish empire.[97]

The crucial events to consider to contextualize the action of this character are the consequences of the French defeat in the fifth Italian war. After the loss of the Duchy of Milan, Francis I singles out the Turk as the sole strong actor who could impinge on a balance of power which in Europe is now decidedly in favour of Charles V. Also to be borne in mind is the impact of military defeats on the internal situation, namely the decimation of the

---

97 See, for instance, Benoit Marechaux, "Business Organisation in the Mediterranean Sea: Genoese Galley Entrepreneurs in the Service of the Spanish Empire (Late Sixteenth and Early Seventeenth Centuries)," *Business History*, Published on line: 10 August 2020. As for admiral Andrea Doria, the huge amount of money granted to him by the emperor should have been employed to contrast the French naval mobilization in a period in which Francis I supports the German Protestant League, conquers Guttenberg and turns Marseille into a safe heaven for Muslim corsairs (1530–1534). See, Aurelio Espinosa, "The Grand Strategy of Charles V (1500–1558); Castile, War, and Dynastic Priority in the Mediterranean," *Journal of Early Modern History*, vol. 9, 3–4, 2005, p. 269.

French ruling class on the battlefields. Hence a new generation of diplomats and advisors may appear on the domestic and international scene thanks to the wise protection granted by Louise of Savoy who controls the bulk of state affairs.[98]

Louise is unpopular and devoid of an army. Nonetheless, she succeeds in resuming relations with the main European powers who were watching with increasing preoccupation the Spanish preponderance. One of the first steps in this strategy was to send da Passano to the English court as her trusted men, and the skilful transactor does not betray the expectations of the French king's mother. As already noted, Henry VIII does agree to a peace treaty with France for which he also receives a considerable monetary payoff.

Another achievement of the ambassador materializes sometimes later, on the Turkish side despite the split at the French court between two parties: the "Evangelic" one favourable to a compromise with Protestants, and the other who advocated an entente with the Habsburg.[99] At first, the Evangelic preponderance materializes in a project of alliance with both the Protestants and the Ottomans to be dealt with

---

98  Alonge, "Evangelismo e ortodossia," p. 1–2.

99  In the coming years, the foreign policy of the French Kingdom would maintain a stance of frontal opposition to Charles V by resorting, on and off, to alliances with schismatic, heretics, and infidels according to the prevalence at court of the 'evangelic' party or the anti-evangelic one favourable to an entente with the Absburg (see, Edith Garnier, *Guillaume du Bellay. L'ange gardien de François Ier*, Paris, Du Felin, 2016). As Alonge points out, what emerges from the French-Turkish relationshipin the first half of the XVI century is a clear correlation between the religious politics of Francis I and his diplomatic strategies. An anti-imperial policy direction based on an alliance with the schismatic England of Henry VIII, the German protestant princes, and the Turk remains in constant opposition to

by the Valois envoy, Antonio Rincon, to Constantinople. The strategy anticipated a French attack in Northern Italy and a simultaneous Turkish offensive against the Spanish possessions in Southern Italy. However, the political balance changes in the meantime at the court of Valois; the project is then abandoned, and the relations with Constantinople cool down.

At this juncture da Passano, despite his old age, enters again into the play with his network of relations. Francis I sends him back to Constantinople whereby, along with Rincon, he must favour a rapprochement between Venetians and Ottomans, and prepare a naval expedition of the Turks against the Spanish fleet. The project of coordinated action between French and Ottomans was just a step away from its implementation when the killing of Rincon by agents of the Duchy of Milan brings the plan to failure. The envoys of Francis I will only succeed in delaying

---

any search of an understanding with the emperor. But the relative strength of the two geopolitical stances would depend on the shifting favour of the king for his advisors. The same kind of divergence was present on the Spanish side as well, but in this case it revolved around Charles' dynastic strategy, on the one hand, and the nationalist agenda of the Castilian clerical elite on the other. Basically, the emperor was focused much more on the reconstruction of a religious unity in Europe than on the Muslim enemy. The Talvera government (1524–1539) was instead contrary to an all-out war against Muslim, Protestant powers and France insofar as it wanted to protect the Spanish trade in the Mediterranean and the coalescing transatlantic economy. Moreover, the government foresaw a disastrous result of the war against the 'heretics', and was in favour of a religious settlement with the Protestant princes almost anticipating the peace of Augsburg of 1555. See, Aurelio Espinosa, "The Grand Strategy of Charles V", p. 242.

the signing of a peace agreement between the Ottomans and the emperor Charles V.[100]

Guillome Alonge concludes his study with some valuable insights on Gioachino da Passano and his branched network of relations. This diplomat frequently acted as a shadow-ambassador who managed the relationships between the French court and the Genoese families who remained loyal to it, in Genoa and other Italian states. Second, his strategy has always been that of pushing Genoa toward an alliance with Henry VIII, the Protestant princes and Suleiman in view of a war against the Spanish emperor, which he deemed inevitable. Third, Alonge points to the ambassador's closeness to the Evangelic milieus and to sympathizers of the Reform, and poses the following question. This biography, as that of other diplomats of that time, might be read through the lenses of *Realpolitik*, that is, it was the pluriconfessional foreign policy of the French kings that pushed them to look for more detached and unconventional state officials. But the hypothesis may also be that religious convictions and diplomatic strategies had influenced one another to bring about tolerant behaviours that underpinned the career of that individuals. Be that as it may, the Ligurian gentleman that emerges from the correspondence with Francis I appears as "a clever observer of the reality of his time, an insightful interpreter of future imperial plays, and a precious advisor for the various French ambassadors in the lagoon city."[101]

In the years of his retirement, Gioachino does not lose his innate propensities. In fact, his will shows that his salient personality traits included familiarity with the practical problems of life and insight into their economic and financial aspects. He had demonstrated these propensities in his early experience

---

100  Alonge, "Evangelismo e ortodossia," p. 2.
101  Ibid., p. 10.

as a merchant, and is doing the same now through a complex mechanism (*moltiplico)* he devised for the multiplication until a distant future of his shares bequeathed by the Bank of Saint George.[102]

102 Giuseppe Felloni, "I molteplici di Gioachino da Passano," in Lercari, *Tra grande patriziato e notabilato locale,* vol. II, pp. 645–666.

# Chapter Five   Entrepreneurship and institutions: Lessons from the case

**Abstract:**

The two characters depicted in the present study came from two neighbour coastal communities which represent well the more advanced part of the Genoese *dominio* with their socio-economic structure so intertwined with that of the capital city. These two socio-economic actors are neither the "exceptional-typical" individuals of Italian microhistory,[103] nor the "cultural

---

103   Carlo Ginsburg, *Il formaggio e i vermi. Il cosmo di un mugnaio del '500*, Torino, Einaudi, 1976; *Idem*, "Microhistory: Two or Three Things That I Know about It," in *Critical Inquiry*, vol. 10, no. 1, 1993, pp. 10–35; Giovanni Levi, *L'eredità immateriale. Carriera di un esorcista nel Piemonte del Seicento*, Milano, Il Saggiatore, 1985. Levi referred to the story of Ginsburg's miller as a fringe case that, thanks to its exceptional nature, allows us to acknowledge that individuals had in the past much more possibilities of thinking and acting than the normative systems of their times and our preconceptions would make us think. (Giovanni Levi, "Les usages de la biographie," in *Annales E.S.C.»*, 44 no. 6, 1989, pp. 1325–1336). A recent reassessment of these seminal works has been proposed by Sabina Loriga who sees them as attempts to overcome the contrast between approaches focused on influential personalities and a social history that insists on the impersonal dimension. Levi has tried to overcome this contradiction by introducing the individual into the social, even if the individuality was that of modest figures who depended on other individuals and institutions. Yet, despite the incapacity to govern the situation, the social action of these individuals is not always irrelevant. Poking around "the interstices of the past", Levi shows that a unitary normative structure able to govern the whole of social

mediators" of global microhistory.[104] They are representatives of a social group of "specialists" and intermediaries who began their careers as merchants, but worked later on at the service

---

experience does not exist. Political powers, markets, communities and the village are not closed systems: all these normative systems leave gaps open in which individual and social groups can act strategically and leave an imprint on political reality. Thus, according to Loriga, people who act within the different systems are social actors who allow overcoming the contrast between glorification and humiliation of subjectivity. And their biographies may permit historians to highlight how they "shape and modify power relations, whether they 'make' history or not" (Sabina Loriga, "The Plurality of the Past: Historical Time and the Rediscovery of Biography," p. 39, in Hans Renders et al. (eds.), *The Biographical Turn. Lives in History*, London, Routledge, 2017; *Idem*, "Negli interstizi della storia," in Paola Lanaro (ed.), *Microstoria. A venticinque anni da L'eredità immateriale*, Milano, Franco Angeli, 2011.

104 This stream of research arises from a debate on how the meaning of microhistory has changed and what it can provide nowadays in front of a global turn in the practice of historical writing. In her reassessment of that debate, Francesca Trivellato highlights that the potential of a micro historical approach to global history has been increasingly exploited from the early 1980s on. In fact, the idea was that biographical studies of individuals and groups that had crossed linguistic, political and religious borders could find a solid base at the micro level to delineate the entanglement of cultural traditions brought about by contacts and clashes among societies after the European expansion of the sixteenth century (Francesca Trivellato, "Is There a Future for Italian Microhistory in the Age of Global History?" *California Italian Studies*, vol. 2, no. 1, 2011). A typical example here of this kind of biographical approach is, Tonio Andrade, "A Chinese Farmer, Two Black Boys, and a Warlord: Towards a Global Microhistory," *The Journal of World History*, vol. 21, no. 4, 2011) in which microhistory becomes

of kings and popes in a historical juncture which brings about relevant changes in the composition of the ruling class of the city-state, especially from 1470 through 1528.[105] Hence, a further step is needed to turn the original descriptive case into an interpretive one. To adequately frame these examples of biography in history, the research stream to bring into the fore is not much microhistory (local or global) as that on the patterns of social advancement in medieval and early modern Italy. This chapter sketches a few features that bear upon the question of how to define our two forms of entrepreneurial agency, and the relationships they were involved in during various stages in their global lives.

---

global by inserting global themes in its narrative. In this research, the multiple connections across cultures and groups are traced from the perspective of involved actors rather than the structures in which such connections take place. Yet, such a perspective is framed by the 'clash of civilization' thesis so that the problem of structure is set aside along with that of the generalization we may draw from a single case. Trivellato addresses the same theme, but sees a future for global microhistory in studies focused on the communication and negotiation channels used by actors who acts as "cultural interpreters" who are not the "modest figures" of the early Italian microhistory. She also points to another possible way to integrate micro and global history which was proposed by Emma Rotschild in her *The Inner Life of Empires* (2011) in which cross-cultural encounters figure prominently, but are not the sole concern, as in most of the micro-histories with a global reach. The invigorating possibility of what Rothschild terms "a new kind of microhistory" is to connect micro- and macro histories by the history of the individuals' own connections".

105 See Jacques Heers p. 328), who defines as "new patrimonies" this group of technicians, mediators, insurance agents, bankers and, mostly, notaries in which he includes Bartolomeo da Framura.

**Key words:** Oligarchic closure, social advancement, entrepreneurs and principals, skilful transactors, weak state, dual polity, private orders, local communities

## 5.1. Notes on oligarchic closure and social mobility in early modern Genoa

Indeed, the  stream of historical research on social mobility proves of high heuristic validity to addresses crucial issues worthy of further elaboration. How did mobility channels such as Church, officialdom, trade, law or diplomacy contribute to shaping the many variables at play in the careers of the two key actors? What were the dynamics of social advancement in their city-state and beyond? The underlying trend emerging from the historical research on social mobility may be sketched as follows.[106]

From the mid-14th century on, the common trend in the Italian states is that social advancement of individuals begins to depend less and less on the economic and demographic growth and more and more on the service to princes or state and communal administrations. This long-lasting trend gets two competing explanations of what was going to happen in

---

106  Sandro Carocci (ed.), *La mobilità sociale nel medioevo*, Roma, Viella, 2010; Lorenzo Tanzini and Sergio Tognetti (eds.), *La mobilità sociale nel Medioevo italiano. Competenze, conoscenze e saperi fra professioni e ruoli sociali*, Viella, 2016; Andrea Gamberini (ed.), *La mobilità sociale nel Medioevo italiano. Stato e istituzioni (secoli XIV-XV)*, Viella, 2017; Sandro Carocci and Isabella Lazzarini (eds.), *Social Mobility in Medieval Italy (1100-1500)*, Viella, 2017; Simone Collavini and Giuseppe Petralia (eds.), *La mobilità sociale nel Medioevo italiano. Cambiamento economico e dinamiche sociali* (secoli XI-XV), Viella, 2020.

local societies in the aftermath of the feudal crisis. The first is in terms of an "oligarchic closure" which rules out almost any chance of social mobility outside the professional group, usually within a polity torn apart by factional fighting. The second sees instead the outcomes of that crisis in terms of rising to power of a "urban proto-bourgeois class", especially in the hubs of economic development and international trade such as Genoa, for instance. This chapter highlights some relevant lessons that can be gleaned from the historical research on social mobility and entrepreneurship to conceptualize forms of agency of upwardly mobile actors who – as the two depicted here – are neither "heroes" nor "modest figures."

Recent developments in historical research on social mobility provide at least three lessons that corroborate what emerges from the present case study. First, the "exogenous" forms of mobility must be framed within the critical junctures of history that bring about the conquest or loss of new dominions and commercial outposts. Second, the forms of mobility linked to individual choices must be related to both the political clout of the subjects involved, and the possession of competences that favour the development of social skills and relations. Third, competences and relations of many members of the proto-bourgeois class allow them to search for eminence also beyond the social space whereby the initial springboard of their career did materialize.

Bartolomeo da Framura and Gioachino da Passano lived in a time which was not only that of oligarchic consolidation. That was also the time in which the city-state was coming across two divides: the external one in the Mediterranean world, and the inner one within its own polity economy. The first divide increasingly materializes in a stiffening of the cultural and political borders between Spain and the Christendom on one side, and the Muslim world on the other. The main implication of that process that led to this Mediterranean divide was a cumulative divergence between the Habsburg and Ottoman empires.[107]

The essential traits of that Mediterranean divide have been highlighted by Aurelio Espinosa in his analysis focused on the grand strategy of Charles V and the reasons why the emperor was somewhat "forgetful" of that frontier. In short, the Protestant Reformation forced Charles to assess his priorities according to the leading idea of religious unity and his dynastic claim of universal monarchy. The Spanish administration, for its part, failed to convince Charles to focus instead on the Muslim enemy in order to protect the coalescing transatlantic system and establish commercial networks of Spanish businessmen. Hence, Charles' ambition would, in the end, compromise Spain's entrepreneurial agenda of defending the Mediterranean against the Ottomans, and – with solid support by the Genoese – the naval mobilization of France.[108] Yet, this is the critical geopolitical juncture in which Genoa emerges as one of the hubs of economic development in the Italian peninsula. And this is the backdrop which reveals the usefulness of comparing agency and relationships of our two characters with those of socio-economic actors operating in the "coalescing transatlantic system."

As for the changes in the polity economy of Genoa and other Italian states, it was already back in the early 14th century that wealth accumulation through economic activities was no longer the main way to social advancement. From then on, the more enterprising merchants, financiers and notaries increasingly tend

---

107   Andrew Hess, *The Forgotten Frontier.* p. 207.

108   Aurelio Espinosa, "The Grand Strategy of Charles V: *Journal of Early Modern History*, vol. 9, no. 3–4, 2005, pp. 239–242; 269–278.

to leave the economic sector to put themselves at the service of princes and administrations that control a growing amount of economic and political resources.[109] This is a historical turn which got two different interpretations. On the one hand, that shift is conceived of in terms of an "oligarchic closure" which stokes factional fighting in most of Italian communes,[110] and has a negative impact on the mobility within professional groups.[111] On the other, that change in the social history of late-Medieval Italy is thought up as the driver of a process that turns a merchant class into an "urban proto-bourgeoisie" of sort.[112]

---

109  This is the synthesis Sandro Carocci makes of the first wave of research on social mobility in Medieval Italy; see, "Introduzione: la mobilità sociale e la 'congiuntura del 1300.' Ipotesi, metodi di indagine, storiografia," 2010, pp. 1–37.

110  Paolo Cammarosano, "Il ricambio e l'evoluzione dei ceti dirigenti nel corso del XIII secolo," in *Magnati e popolani nell'Italia comunale*, Atti del XV Convegno di studi, Pistoia, 15–18 maggio 1995, pp. 17–40. On the factional fighting in Genoa between 1339 and 1528, when the process of institutional reforms was set in motion by Andrea Doria see, Riccardo Musso, *Lo stato 'cappellazzo'. Genova tra Adorni e Fregosi (1436-1464), Studi di Storia Medioevale e di Diplomatica*, Dipartimento di Scienze della Storia e della Documentazione Storica, Università di Milano", 17, 1988, pp. 223–288; *Idem*, "El stato nostro de Zenoa". Aspetti istituzionali della prima dominazione sforzesca su Genova (1464–78). *Serta Antiqua et Mediaevalia*, no. 5, 2001, pp. 199–236.

111  See, Donata Degrassi, "Il mondo dei mestieri artigianali," in Sandro Carocci (ed.), 2010, pp. 273–287.

112  Petralia, in his analysis on the social advancement of medieval merchants draws from the classic works on the crisis of feudal society and the emergence of an urban proto-bourgeois class such as, Henri Pirenne, *Storia economica e sociale del Medioevo, italiano*, Garzanti, 1975 [1963]; Roberto S. Lopez, *La rivoluzione commerciale nel Medioevo*, Torino, Einaudi, 1975 and, Carlo

Hereinafter, some references will be made to the second kind of interpretation which finds more feedback in medieval and early modern Genoa, and calls for a deepening of the investigation of the links between  patterns of social advancement and the spatial mobility of individuals and families.[113] On this the point is made by Giuseppe Petralia: the acquisition of eminence within the urban space is important for merchants and financiers. But it is not to be taken as their exclusive aim:

> "The scene and world of long-distance networks, the action and time spent in the hubs of capital cities, diasporas, and the big Mediterranean and European merchants squares, were going to open other frontiers and build up other life programmes. The investment on the political scene of the homeland might even fade in front of a direct engagement with the big merchandise, and even more so in front of the service in courts and state administrations if these pointed to the access routes to bureaucratic roles or noble ranks."[114]

This is precisely what happened to our characters – and others similar to them – in Renaissance Genoa. Yet, the attempt to define these middle-range forms of agency also implies a degree of multidisciplinary openness which is in fact apparent in the historical research on social mobility. An example is a methodological suggestion that can be drawn from a re-reading of Pitirim Sorokin's classic work on mobility channels within a

---

M. Cipolla, *Storia economica dell'Europa preindustriale*, Bologna, Il Mulino, 2002.

113　Petralia in Carocci (ed.), 2010, p. 250.

114　Ibid., p. 263. The same point is made by Vittorio Tigrino when he emphasizes the need to investigate on those wide reaching external relations that communities, social groups and individual actors have the capacity to push for outside the Genoese range. (Vittorio Tigrino, "Il dibattito storico-politico sul Dominio della Repubblica

multidimensional vision of the social space in which they take shape. These channels are institutions which favour the passage of an individual from one social position to another. Family, kinship, school, bureaucracy, military, political and professional organizations -all operate to a different degree in promoting social advancement.[115] Sandro Carocci, who proposes the re-reading, points out that such a notion may be applied to the Middle Ages as well, but the accepted meaning of institution should be more "loose" to include, for instance, informal and patron-client relations.[116]

A second insight from re-reading Sorokin is that the individual place in a system of social standing stems from the set of roles played in different economic, political and professional domains which are often interrelated, even if imperfectly.[117] On this,

---

di Genova in età moderna: feudi, ex-feudi, città e quasi-città," in *Libertà e dominio*, s.d. Ricerche DHL, 6, bozza 1, pp. 315–66.

115 Pitirim A. Sorokin, *Social Mobility*, Routledge Thoemmes Press, 1998, [1927], chapter VIII: pp. 164–181.

116 Carocci (2010), pp. 11–13.

117 As For the way to define social spaces, Carocci refers to Bourdieu's distinction between three forms of capital that in combination can determine individual social positions. In Bourdieu's words: "Depending on the field in which it functions, and the cost of a more or less expensive transformations which are the precondition for its efficacy in the field in question, capital can present itself in three fundamental guises: as economic capital, which is immediately and directly convertible into money and may be institutionalized in the form of property rights; as cultural capital, which is convertible, in certain conditions, into economic capital and may be institutionalized in the form of educational qualifications; and as social capital, made up of social obligations ('connections'), which is convertible, in certain conditions, into economic capital and may be institutionalized in the form of a title of nobility." (Pierre Bourdieu, *The Forms of Capitalism* in

Carocci notes that the emphasis on the composite character of social stratification makes the medievalist aware of how complex the task is to spell out the processes of social change: "A precise measurement of social mobility looks increasingly difficult even to sociologists (...) that in some cases come to prefer a qualitative approach to social mobility and base their appraisals, just as medievalists, on biography and family events."[118]

More recent studies provide suggestions on some relatively neglected issues in previous works such as, for instance, the cultural facets of mobility and their role in shaping new social identities.[119] On the cause of this neglect, the hypothesis has been advanced that a sheer adoption of cultural patterns of dominant classes was the normal behaviour of those who did aspire to social recognition.[120] Thus, the suggestion is that noble behavioural patterns,

> Would have triggered imitative processes among successful citizen-businessmen unable to give shape to a class culture suitable for changing society in a capitalist sense, but able instead to use their wealth to get co-opted into the dominant classes according to methods and forms of nobility. Generations of merchants would have been followed by

---

John Richardson, *Handbook of Theory and Research for the Sociology of Education*, Greenwood, 1986, pp. 241–258.

118  Carocci, 2010, p. 15.

119  As Isabella Lazzarini notes, dealing with social mobility implies facing up to a complex field of investigation which includes many relevant features of the social space such as merchandising, offices, reputation, worldliness, political information and access to power. ("Mercatura e diplomazia: itinerari di mobilità sociale nelle élite italiane (qualche esempio fiorentino, XV secolo)," in Tanzini e Tognetti, 2016: p. 2).

120  Ibid.

others of rent-seekers which would have outnumbered those of merchants.[121]

In his reassessment of that thesis, Sergio Tognetti recalls the fundamentals as they presented themselves between the second half of the 14th and the end of the 15th century, and that seems not to validate the correlation between the oligarchic closure and the turning of career persons into rent-seekers. The research evidence shows that despite scattered signs of decay, Italy kept its primacy in manufacturing, trade and finance well beyond the Late Middle Ages.[122]

As for Genoa, Tognetti starts from this leading idea. The impossibility of building a wide dominion in the hinterland to underpin institutional support to its businessmen may have been the root cause of the spread of multiple forms of entrepreneurial creativity and adaptability. Some of these forms (recalled in Chapter Two) include: the reorientation of long-distance trade from the Islamic Mediterranean and the Slavic Black Sea toward the Atlantic in the aftermath of the Ottoman expansion; the merchant associations  known as *maone* as precursors, in a sense, of modern cartels; the contracting out to the Bank of Saint George of fiscal policy at the outset, and the government of territories later on; the flourishing of silk and wool industries, and the persistent financial power of the Genoese bankers. Also to be added is the ability of aristocratic families undergoing a

---

121  Sergio Tognetti, "Uomini d'affari e mobilità sociale in Italia tra metà del Trecento e primo Cinquecento," *Estratto da Archivio Storico Italiano*,1. a. 175 no. 651, 2017, p. 120.

122  For instance, Tognetti points out that the huge amount of investments in land from the end of the 15th century onwards was often aimed at the betterment of farming in a primary sector which promised conspicuous returns.

decay of their political power to offset this liability with a greater engagement in economic activities. And finally, the spread of extended groups gathering nobles and non-nobles families (*alberghi*) that acted as legitimized channels for the co-optation into the higher ranks of the Genoese polity.[123]

The evidence gathered in those domains shows that the "oligarchic closure" is a thesis at least ahead of time insofar as it advances – of at least a century – a set of social dynamics which are traced back to it. In other words, reading the outcomes of that trend as rent-seeking thriving and entrepreneurship smothering seems the outcome of an anti-elitist approach. In fact, the neglected issue is that of defining and measuring the threshold of political representation of a social structure below which one can speak of oligarchy.[124]

To sum up, the historical studies on social mobility referred to here show that the political element certainly becomes increasingly important, but this does not imply that a process of oligarchic closure had been unfolding that stifled economic activities and fuelled rent-seeking. On the contrary, the political factor became a driver of social mobility in three respects. The first relates to the "external" mobility driven by conquests, construction of dominions and creation of colonial government

---

123 Tognetti, 2017, pp. 138–140. See also, among others, Rodolfo Savelli, *La repubblica oligarchica. Legislazione, istituzioni e ceti a Genova nel Cinquecento*, Milano, Giuffrè Editore, 1981; Edoardo Grendi, *La repubblica aristocratica dei genovesi*, Bologna Il Mulino, 1987; the two chapters by Carlo Bitossi, "L'età di Andrea Doria" and "La Repubblica di Genova: politica e istituzioni," in Giovanni Assereto e Marco Doria (eds.), *Storia della Liguria*, Bari, Laterza, 2007, and Arturo Pacini, "I presupposti politici del 'secolo dei genovesi': la riforma del 1528," in *Atti della Società Ligure di Storia Patria*, XXX, no. 1, 1990.

124 Tognetti, 2017, p. 14.

structures. The second concern the social advancement favoured by the "proximity to rule", that is, the capacity of weaving relations with power holders brought about by specific professional skills or social attitudes such as those developed in court environments. The proof of this may be found in the huge number of businessmen that princes all over Europe involved as money lenders, advisors, ambassadors and top civil servants.

Actually, the two biographies sketched here, and others one may find in the literature, show that the service to kings and popes does not necessarily mean becoming a rent seeker.[125] It may mean, instead, going ahead with economic activities or becoming a political entrepreneur in other institutional contexts. "[126] Thus

---

125 Alberto Luongo, "Notariato e mobilità sociale nell'Italia cittadina del XIV secolo," in Tanzini and Tognetti, 2016, pp. 243–272; Isabella Lazzerini, "Mercatura e diplomazia," in idem, 2016, pp. 273–298. This second study provides two examples of social advancement one of whom shows not a few similarities with the career path of Gioachino da Passano in a context also similar in its combination of the trading and financial calling with the exercise of public functions. The career patterns of two Florentine ambassadors described in that study are further proofs that competence and knowledge coming from merchandise, the attitude to communication, and the control of political information were the privileged channels of access to diplomacy and, at the same time an asset to build up own social and political eminence.

126 In the collective work on social mobility in the middle ages, one may find a study by Donata Degrassi on the mining enterprises in different areas of the Italian peninsula. This study provides scattered evidence on the skilled workforce, the patterns of recruitment, and also on the relationships between the mining activity and social mobility. And finally, it sketches a profile of Tommaso Marinai, a man with a career patterns similar to that of Bartolomeo da Framura. "Issued from a family of middle social status and low income, Tommaso succeed, thanks to his

we need to spell out where and when and how the premises of self-fulfilment do materialize. Useful in this regard are the outcomes of case studies that investigate how economic actors move back and forth between organizational and institutional settings in a given socio-economic environment. This applies, for instance, to "Atlantic entrepreneurs" of the XVI and XVII centuries with their diversified talents and multiplicity of career patterns.

Matteo Salonia provides some examples of these transprofessional and transnational careers of individuals who exemplify the maritime tradition and cosmopolitan culture brought by the Genoese into the Atlantic. Among these examples, one may single out the story of Giovanni Pastene, who started as a navigator, but soon began to rise in the Spanish imperial ranks whereby he got the military title of *teniente general* and also improved his socio-economic position with that of *encomendero*. Another example of how diversified the Genoese activities in the New World were is Augustin Justiniano, a merchant who quickly seized the opportunity to buy and exploit a silver mine for three decades.

---

> knowledge of mining, to become a young founder, financier and director of enterprise. The dissolution of this establishment to create a new consortium gave a thrust to his career thanks to the partnership with people located at the higher echelons of society. His gains as director of the new mine, along with those he received as shareholder allowed him to invest in land and real estate in the vicinity of the mine. His reputation, and the high level of his competences favoured his approaching to the higher level of political power so that he became the counsellor of Lorenzo de Medici on mining issues. (Donata de Grassi, "L'impresa mineraria nel Medioevo: competenze tecniche, organizzazione, mobilità geografica e sociale," in Tanzini e Tognetti (ed.) *La mobilità sociale nel Medioevo*, p. 28.

The analytical framework of these case studies has been aimed at clarifying the links between human action, civic culture and institutions through a focus on the multiplicity, and often the simultaneity of careers. Thus the emphasis is both on how the Genoese adapted to the economic challenges in the new kingdoms of America, and how they used the institutional tools of the Castillian colonies to further their integration in those societies.[127] However, in the present study the attention is focused not so much on the multiplicity of careers as a leverage of socio-cultural integration. Rather the focus is on the turning point when the multiplicity of trades ends, and the economic actor turns into an institutional entrepreneur in a specific organizational context. Hence, other interpretive cases may be taken as more insightful comparators to grasp the relationships between our two entrepreneurial agents and their principals.

In the most recent of those studies, Kaarle Wirta addresses "a transatlantic world of cross-cultural practices" mainly based on the reports from a manager of various West India companies to the European headquarters. His approach builds on theories of microhistory to show how the idea of "Circum-Atlantic" incorporates the typical transprofessional career of Henrich Carloff who played the roles of director, investor, commander, and governor. Wirta conceptualizes the Atlantic entrepreneur within the "exceptional-typical" duality, often used in microhistory, for exceptional was Carloff's invaluable experience, and typical was the way he managed his company. Then Wirta reaches out to a social-scientific perspective by emphasizing the social underpinnings of entrepreneurship: experience, personal networks, trust and reputation and concludes that the narrative he provides depicts individual careers that typify "middle-range

---

127  Matteo Salonia, *Genoa's Freedom*, pp. 148–150; 154–155.

forms of agency" of people who were creative in the management of companies established in Europe and managed overseas.[128]

The same type of conduct and context had been examined thirty years earlier by Ann Carlos and Stephen Nicholas, but through different analytical lenses. While Wirta emphasizes the social (relational) capital of an Atlantic entrepreneur, these authors addressed instead organizational issues such as how managerial hierarchies economized on transaction cost and how the European headquarters controlled local managers. Their main finding was that the five companies in their sample were managed more or less efficiently according to their capacity to deal with the problem of control from the headquarters. Carlos and Nicholas conceptualize this as the "agency problem". Given that the most detailed contract between the "principals" in Europe and agents on the spot could not specify all the actions to take in every contingency, the *costs of agency* kept being high. Despite the available ways to reduce transaction costs (indents,

---

128 Kaarle Wirta, "Rediscovering Agency in the Atlantic. A Biographical Approach Linking Entrepreneurial Spirit and Overseas Companies," in Hans Renders, Binne de Haan and Jonne Harsma (eds.), *The Biographical Turn. Lives in History*, London, Routledge, 2017, pp. 118–120, 124–128. *Idem, Early Modern Overseas Trade and Entrepreneurship: Nordic Trading Companies in the Seventeenth Century*, Routledge, 2020. Wirta draws from studies of micro historians on the spatial and temporal aspects of the micro-macro link. Pointedly, he refers to the degree of openness to the other social sciences that transpires in the "method of clues" and its focus on a peculiar event as a sign of a wider structure that needs to be explained. See, Matti Peltonen, "Clues, Margins and Monads: The Micro-Macro Link in Historical Research," *History and Theory*, XL 2001, 349–351. Ann M. Carlos and Stephen Nicholas, "Giants of an Earlier Capitalism: The Chartered Trading Companies as Modern Multinational," *Business History Review*, vol. LXII, 1988, pp. 398–419.

committees, rules of procurement), the problem of "managing the managers" was there to stay.[129]

The third study on the same subject proposes further explanations of the scarce effectiveness in managing local managers. The authors, S.R.H. Jones and Simon Ville,[130] did not see the vertical integration of production as more effective than a coalition of franchisees as a means to reduce transaction costs. In their view, such a comparatively inefficient transaction mode was preferred for two reasons. First, it was a source of monopoly rents for courtiers and other shareholders in Europe. Second, it was a tool to project the power of Mercantilist states. That is why the divergence between organizational aims and practices persisted along with a good deal of window dressing in reports to the headquarters. Jones and Ville also note that Carlos and Nicholas study "made too much of company culture" for they noticed scant evidence of corporate culture in a "self-serving and cosmopolitan staff" of West India companies.[131] A staff made of "skillful transactors" that had to interact with "rent-seeking monopolists," and were themselves rent-seekers to some extent.

Atlantic entrepreneurs are good comparative references to highlight the agency of their Genoese counterparts. This prompt the question: Are the emphasis on socio-cultural underpinnings of entrepreneurial actions and the exceptional-typical duality

---

129  The conflict of interest between managers and shareholders was addressed by Carlos and Nicholas also in, "Agency Problems in Early Chartered Companies: The Case of the Hudson Bay Company," *The Journal of Economic History*, vol. 50, no. 4, 1990, pp. 853–875.

130  S.R. H. Jones and Simon P. Ville, "Efficient Transactors or Rent-Seeking Monopolists? The Rationale for Early Chartered Trading Companies," *The Journal of Economic History*, LVI, 1996, pp. 898–915.

131  Ibid.

the best ways to conceptualize the relations between principals and "assigned" entrepreneur? I surmise that in a polity whereby economic and institutional actions often intermingle, they are not. The transprofessional careers of our cosmopolitan actors point at their quality of skilful transactors and fixers, able to widen the context and upgrade the original economic content of their transactions in their paths of social advancement.

The approach to the history-biography link has been applied in this case along three steps of a casing process in an attempt to transform the initial description of two global lives into an analytical explanation of what this case is a case of. In other words, the aim of the study was to highlight the causal pathways that shaped the two forms of entrepreneurial agency focused upon. The first step of the casing process was to go beyond the initial description of the socio-economic dynamics of a local community in search of clues from Genoese history that could help trace the causal processes at play in the career paths of our key actors. The second one was to highlight the limited heuristic value of microhistorical and cultural approaches for the theory development of an interpretive case. The third step -expounded in what follows is to devise an analytical vocabulary to put forward middle-range generalizations on the entrepreneurial action of the two "agents with causal capacities" examined here.[132]

---

132  On how to make theory development out of a descriptive case see, Alexander George and Andrew Bennet, *Case Studies and Theory Development in the Social Science*, Boston, MIT Press, 2005. See also, Pascal Venesson, "Case Studies and Process Tracing: Theories and Practices," in Donatella della Porta and Michael Keating (eds.), *Approaches and Methodologies in the Social Sciences: A Pluralist Perspective*, Cambridge University Press, 2008, pp. 223–239; Andrew Schrank, "Essentials for the Case Study Method. The Case Study and Causal Inference," in Ellen Perecman and Sara

New insights to advance in this direction may be found, bearing in mind this point. Early modern Genoa was going to play a crucial role in the Spanish Atlantic, but kept the so-called Feudal Mountain in its backstage. This inner divide should be given due attention to better understand the working of "a minimal state" that Bartolomeo da Framura and Gioachino da Passano served in the early stages of their transnational careers.

As Oliver Williamson points out, in his taking stock of transaction cost economics, the institutional environment is partly shaped by evolutionary processes, but sometimes may be changed by design through the definition and enforcement of property rights and contract laws. However, cumulative changes of progressive kind are difficult to orchestrate because of both internal and external shocks. Wars, occupations or institutional breakdown may bring about breaks from the established procedure. Thus, such "defining moments" may sometimes open up windows of opportunity to effect broad reforms.[133] Actually, the defining moment of 1528–1576 did not open up many opportunities for broad structural changes in the Genoese polity economy in the period under consideration. To clarify this, the case suggests that we should relate

---

R. Curran (eds.), *A Handbook for Social Science Field Research*, Thousand Oaks, Sage, 2006; Elina Pernu, "The Process of Casing in Business Studies –The Impact of Researcher's Sense Making," *Third Annual IMP Conference*, KEDGE Business School, Bordeaux, September 6, 2014, pp. 1–13.

133 Oliver Williamson, "The Evolving Science of Organization," *Journal of Institutional and Theoretical Economics*, vol. 149, no. 1, 1993, pp. 36–63. See also, Geoffrey Hodgson, *How Economics Forgot History: The Problem of Historical Specificity in Social Science*, New York, Taylor & Francis, 2001, in which the history to retrieve is German historicism with its crucial role in laying the foundations of institutional economics.

cognition and self-interestedness of socio-economic actors – in a polity with a transactional focus – to the long-standing "executive powerlessness" of the Genoese state which made the implementation of policies quite problematic.[134]

Indeed, Genoese rulers proved quite creative in coping with the problem of their scant capacities to enforce the implementation of policies. In the fifteenth century they did find a "functional alternative" in the Bank of Saint George to implement one policy first and all the policies where it was needed later on. In terms of Williamson's framework, this means that representatives of both the institutional and private ordering – in what was dubbed as the "corporate city" – reached a "make-or-buy" type of agreement on fiscal policies and the management of public debt.[135]

The defining moment of making the first-order choice of putting the formal rules of the game right arrives anyhow in that critical juncture of 1528–1576 when an attempt is really made to centralize the state administration. An attempt that will be put to test by the inner dualism between a city which was a hub of economic development and a hinterland with vestiges of feudalism.[136]

---

134 Giovanni Assereto, *Le metamorfosi della repubblica* Savona, Elio Ferraris Editore, 2000; Edoardo Grendi, *Il Cervo e la repubblica. Il modello ligure di antico regime*, Einaudi, 1993; Carlo Bitossi, *Il governo dei magnifici. Patriziato e politica a Genova fra Cinque e Seicento*, Genova, ECIG, 1990; Carlo Bitossi, "La Repubblica di Genova: politica e istituzioni," in Giovanni Assereto and Marco Marco Doria (ed.) Doria, *Storia della Liguria*, Bari. Laterza, 2007.

135 Giuliano Procacci defined Genoa as a "Corporate city" (*città-azienda*) in, *Storia degli italiani*, vol. 1, Bari Laterza, 1969, and Steven Epstein used the term "corporate state" in, *Genoa and the Genoese, 958-1528*, The University of Carolina Press, 1996.

136 Andrea Zanini, "Strategie politiche ed economia feudale ai confine della Repubblica di Genova, (secoli XVI-XVIII)," *Atti della Società*

All this notwithstanding, an institutional system still weak and quite inefficient gets, again, to the point of equilibrium, this time through dealings not with a group of wealthy merchants, but with local expressions of a private ordering in local communities.[137] Yet, contrary to what happened with the procurement contract with the eight founders of the Bank of Saint George, the priority in the hinterland was not a reduction of transaction costs for the economic and institutional actors involved. Rather, it was the containment of social conflict and autonomist claims that could have put the state borders at risk of foreign invasion. Thus, the priority becomes carrying out law and order in the riotous part of the *dominio* through a more effective criminal justice. But the problem would remain the same – the weak enforcement capacities due to the scarcity of funds to pay magistrates and Corsican soldiers. Given this state of affairs, the point of equilibrium could not be found in the readiness of policy implementation as in the capacity of state officials to grant tutelage, arbitration, and assurance in a social world riddled with conflicts.[138]

Another capacity of these institutional actors is worth noting, though. Social instability in the Feudal Mountain did not materialize just in the guise of factional fighting. Conflicts among kinships (*parentele*) also were endemic, and in not a

---

*Ligure di Storia Patria*, XLV, CXIX, 2005; *Idem*, "Tra pubblico e privato: la politica territoriale della Repubblica di Genova nel Levante Ligure (secoli XVI-XVIII)," Atti del convegno di studi, *Feudi di Lunigiana tra Impero, Spagna e Stati Italiani*, a cura di Elena Fasano Guarini e Franco Bonatti, Memorie dell'Accademia Lunigianense di Scienze, vol. LXXVIII, La Spezia, 2007.

137 Osvaldo Raggio, *Faide e parentele. Lo stato genovese visto dalla Fontanabuona,* Torino Einaudi, 1990.

138 Giovanni Assereto, "Le metamorfosi della repubblica," pp. 55, 88–89.

few kinships, one could find smugglers, street bandits, and troublemakers of various sorts often affiliated to factions of different colours. In short, the limited enforcement capacity of an institutional structure was going to find its "functional alternatives" in forms of relational governance stemming from a set of transactions among institutional and social actors. What we have here is another form of indirect government, but this time what is contracted out is the control of previous offenders to their kinship to be ratified in "pacification agreements" in which the kinship engaged itself in cooperating with the judges to give effective implementation to the sentences.[139]

This is then the critical juncture of history in which our two characters lived in a city which emerged from the feudal crisis as one of the hubs of economic development and international trade within the backdrop of the Mediterranean divide. However, the inner divide between an early modern polity economy in the city and the lingering of traits of a feudal society in the Apennines must also be borne in mind. This is a dualism which deserve some thoughts in relation to the failed attempt to build the institutions of a regional state for the aristocratic republic in the making from 1528 through 1576. Hence, it was deemed appropriate to provide some evidence to compare the agency relationships of our upwardly mobile actors also with those of members of the ruling class that upwardly mobile were to a limited extent, and had no better options than to represent the city government in the unruly part of the Genoese *dominio*.

---

139  Osvaldo Raggio, *Faide e parentele*, pp. 12–21.

## Chapter Six    Giving a historical face to entrepreneurship: Issues for debate


**Abstract:**
Historical approaches to social mobility referred to in this study also are social-scientific in character insofar as they account for the composite nature of social stratification within a multidimensional view of the processes that impinge on it. That is why they provide valuable insights to give a historical face to entrepreneurship.

The global lives of Bartolomeo da Framura and Gioachino da Passano confirm the validity of that multidimensional view of social mobility. Actually, their notary, trading, entrepreneurial, military, and diplomatic skills have been applied in various organizational contexts and to the service of powerful institutional "principals." The historical studies on social mobility, with their interdisciplinary bent, have proven to be a suitable backdrop for trying to develop a thought on the two examples of entrepreneurial agency which got embedded in various organizational and institutional contexts overtime. This chapter makes a step ahead in this attempt by confronting responses of scholars raised in the cultural turn with others advanced in the political-economic approach to the "Schumpeter's plea" for historical reasoning on entrepreneurship.[140]


---

140 The responses of business historians to the "Schumpeter's plea" assessed here are especially the following: Daniel Wadhwani and Christina Lubinski, "Reinventing Entrepreneurial History," *The Business History Review*, 91, December 2017, pp. 767–799; Mathias Kipping, Takafumi Kurosawa, and Daniel Wadhwani, "A Revisionist Historiography of Business History: A Richest Past for a Richer Future", in John Wilson, Steven Toms, Abe de Jong,

**Key words:** cultural turn, institutions and entrepreneurship, transactional focus, entrepreneurial history.

## 6.1. Historical thinking on entrepreneurship within the cultural turn

The discussion of the cultural-cognitive replies to Schumpeter's plea advanced here is limited in scope. In fact, what is focused upon are just the research premises of the replies, which allegedly should revitalize the original potential of entrepreneurship studies in business history.

Three are the leading ideas deemed to be relevant for "reinventing" entrepreneurial history in this stream of research. Firstly, to make up for a loss of the temporal foundations

---

and Emily Buchnea (eds.), *The Routledge Companion to Business History*, 2017, pp. 19–35; Daniel Wadhwani, "Entrepreneurship in Historical Context: Using History to Develop Theory and Understand Process," in Friederike Welter and Bill Gartner (eds.), *A Research Agenda for Entrepreneurship and Context*, Cheltenham, Edward Elgar 2016, pp. 65–78; Daniel Wadhwani and Geoffrey Jones, "Schumpeter's Plea: Historical Reasoning in Entrepreneurship Theory and Research," in Marcelo Bucheli and Daniel Wadhwani (eds.), *Organizations in Time: History, Theory and Methods*, Oxford University Press, 2014, pp. 192–216; Daniel Wadhwani "Historical Reasoning on the Development of Entrepreneurship Theory," in Hans Landström and Franz Lohrke (eds.), *Historical Foundations of Historical Research*, Edward Elgar 2010, pp. 343–362; Geoffrey Jones and Daniel Wadhwani, "Entrepreneurial Theory and the History of Globalization," in *Business and Economic History On-Line*, vol. 5, 2007, pp. 1–26; Geoffrey Jones and Daniel Wadhwani, "Entrepreneurship and Business History: Renewing the Research Agenda," *Harvard Business School Working Papers*, no. 07-0007, 2006, pp. 1–49.

of agency with a focus on how entrepreneurs see the future despite the constraints of the present. This does not imply a conceptualization of the future in terms of either "measurable risks or unknowable uncertainties."[141] It implies, instead, a focus on the "entrepreneur's efforts to shape the seemingly unpredictable future through sense-making and rhetorical processes" along with a creative utilization of the past.[142]

This premise, advanced by Daniel Wadhwani and Christina Lubinski, is supposed to render the structural postulation at least incomplete. In other words, what is put into question is the assumption of "old" economic history according to which the choices of actors are predetermined by the institutional context. These authors do not follow William Baumol who focused on the institutional constraints that impinge upon the quality of entrepreneurial agency.[143] They state their intention to follow Schumpeter in his emphasis on "the shaping influence of institutions on entrepreneurship, but also the 'bursting' influence of entrepreneurs on institutions."[144]

For Wadhwani and Lubinki, the manner in which entrepreneurs shape the future is one of the building blocks to address the creative responses these socio-economic actors can provide to historical change. Their approach is focused on entrepreneurial processes, but they state the intention to

---

141  As Frank Knights states in his classic work, *Risk, Uncertainty and Profit*, New York, Dover Publications, 1921 (chapter VII).

142  Wadwani and Lubinski, "Reinventing Entrepreneurial History," pp. 777.

143  William Baumol, "Entrepreneurship: Productive, Unproductive and Destructive," *Journal of Political Economy*, vol. 98, no. 5, 1990, pp. 893–921.

144  Wadhwani and Lubinski, "Reinventing Entrepreneurial History," p. 778.

not exclude individuals and organizations from the study of entrepreneurial processes. Still, a de facto exclusion seems to exist in their approach, considering how they intend the second and third premises for a renewal of the research agenda. In fact, the agency they have in mind is that of human actors who pursue entrepreneurial opportunities through a process in which the values to go after are not solely the economic and commercial ones: they are political, environmental, aesthetic, academic and civic as well. As the two authors state, "the issue of how entrepreneurial actors determine a desirable and plausible future is an empirical one requiring historical research rather than behavioral premises that can be assumed."[145]

The variety of values attached to different opportunities goes along with the distribution of agency among an array of actors over time. The assumption here is that structural and historical change – such as the rise of a big business or the integration of global markets – can only be accounted for by tracing the creative actions of many actors, often as they build upon previous actions or experiences. This research premise contrasts with the treatment of entrepreneurs as heroic individuals, as has sometimes been the case in the historical literature. While the actions of individuals matter, this "reinventing" of entrepreneurial history intends to emphasize the cumulative entrepreneurial processes sometimes referred to as "distributed agency" that propels historical change.

Wadhwani and Lubinski specify that this does not indicate neglect for the explanatory power of biographies which as a genre remain well-positioned to examine concrete and carefully contextualized entrepreneurial processes.[146] However, the two

---

145  Ibid., p. 778.
146  Ibid., p. 779.

authors seem to have no interest in how the agency of a given upwardly mobile (not "heroic") actor is exerted in different times and spaces. The reason for this stance seems to lie in the nature of an approach in which sense-making and the attention to the inner workings of "human action" are deemed the best way "for grappling with the unbearable elusiveness of entrepreneurial opportunities."[147]

These research premises are advanced with the aim to highlight what has supposedly been lost in the reasoning on entrepreneurship in business history, and to retrieve it through interdisciplinary dialogue and a reactivation of the broken links with historicism. The shared view, in this research stream, is that the "Chandlerian turn" toward the study of big firms has oriented business history toward the gathering of evidences on prices, transactions and markets. Hence the claim that entrepreneurship has become a "stifled alternative" which

---

147 Dino Dimov, "Grappling with the Unbearable Elusiveness of Entrepreneurial Opportunities," *Entrepreneurship Theory and Practice*, vol. 35, no. 1, 2011, pp. 57–81. Wadhwani and Lubinski claim that entrepreneurship as a discipline has a long tradition of grappling with the "situated perspective of human actors" in interpreting their motivations and meanings. In this respect they refer to the microhistorical tradition by pointing, for instance, to the work of Giovanni Levi, "Microhistory and the Recovery of Complexity," in Susanna Fellman and Saja Rahikainen (eds.), *Historical Knowledge: In Quest of Theory, Methods and Evidence*, Cambridge Scholars Publishing, 2012. The two authors also refer to many other works focused on the role of emotion; on how sense making in the present impinge on how to look at the future through monologues, dialogues and role playing; on how they legitimate novelty, and how entrepreneurial actors convince others to reallocate resources and reconfigure investments (Wadhwani and Lubinski, "Reinventing Entrepreneurial History," pp. 780–787.

survives in the discipline only in its economic-based versions. The conclusion then is that what has become "intractable" are issues such as agency, perceptions, ways to imagine the future, plurality of motivations, creativity and temporality.[148]

In what follows, I reassess such a claim based on the idea that the case in point suggests an opposite research orientation: to give a historical face to entrepreneurship, one should rethink precisely some of those economic-based versions and the way they treated the demanding issue of entrepreneurial agency.

In their reasoning on the theme, Wadhwani and Jones (2014) elaborate further on the variations of historical contexts which shape the definition and enactment of entrepreneurial opportunities. But in doing so, they reckon business in the making more than the business already running. Consequently, a point is lost in their proposed involvement with historicism: institutions have a bearing on the definition and enactment of entrepreneurial opportunities, but they also impinge upon the transaction costs for those already in business. As a matter of fact, entrepreneurship is far from a stifled alternative in business history, for studies are not lacking that disconfirm such a thesis which seems to come from quite a selective reading of Chandler's works. It is not simply *Strategy and Structure* that matters in the history of economic organizations. His *Scale and Scope* also inspired historical studies on how different institutional contexts impact the costs of doing business.[149]

For instance, in his overview of Genoese history from 958 through 1528 Steven Epstein asks: What were the reasons for

---

148  Ibid., p. 770.

149  Alfred Chandler, *Strategy and Structure: Chapters in the History of the Industrial Empire*, Boston, MIT Press, 1962; *Idem, Scale and Scope: The Dynamics of Industrial Capitalism*, Cambridge Ma., Belknap Press, 1990.

the successes and failures of the Genoese in expanding their trade and increasing their economic prosperity? In late medieval Genoa, the government did not attempt to regulate the economy. Guilds were quite weak forms of organization, as in other port cities.[150] Economic actors did cooperate in the context of family or *alberghi* (aggregation of families).[151] Beyond these domains, business relations were based on reciprocity, arbitration, and written contracts.[152]

To clarify the reasons for the commercial success of the city, Epstein draws on the conceptual coupling of scale and scope borrowed from the history of enterprise by Alfred Chandler. As he explains, the scale of activity keeps growing until the Genoese can increase their allocative efficiency, owing to incentives embodied in contractual agreements that solve, up to a certain extent, the commercial and financial risks in transport and trade. Access to more profitable markets is somewhat assured by the

---

150  Steven Epstein, *Genoa and the Genoese, 958-1528*, The University of Carolina Press, 1996; Luciano Grossi Bianchi and Ennio Poleggi, *Una città portuale nel medioevo: Genova nei secoli X-XVI*, Genova SAGEP, 1987.

151  There are various explanations on the establishment of these federations of families which relate them to the internal discord, in a way or another. For instance, Avner Greif sees the *alberghi* as part of a factionalist dynamics that involved the city clans during the shift from the consulate to the *podesteria* (see, *Institutions and the Path to the Modern Economy: Lessons from Medieval Trade*, Cambridge University Press, 2006, p. 245). A different view –referred to in this study- is proposed by Osvaldo Raggio (1990) who sees the *alberghi* as social and economic forms of organization that acted as functional substitutes for the weakness of state authority.

152  Quentin Van Doosselaere, *Commercial Agreements and Social Dynamics in Medieval Genoa*, Cambridge University Press, 2009.

containment of costs and the acquisition of trade privileges in the destination countries. Regarding the product range (scope), it is quite limited at the outset due to the limited cargo capacities of the galleys, but the next improvement in naval construction makes an increase in scope possible.[153] Epstein adds that the city government can also contribute to the reduction of transaction costs through custom agreements and the acquisition of residential neighbourhoods in many Mediterranean cities. The low cost of notary registration is another influential factor in the containment of transaction costs.

The concepts of scale and scope are also applied by Oscar Gelderblom in his study of the Dutch merchant Hans Thijs in a context whereby combinations of market, enterprise hierarchy, and relational contracting provided the best opportunities for merchants in Amsterdam and Gdansk to tackle problems of agency relationships and information asymmetries.[154] The different dynamism of trade in the two cities is also explained by Ulf Ewert and Stephan Seltzer who focused on the institutions that governed the Hansa League, the network structure which coordinated trade, the risk-avoidance strategies of merchants

---

153  Epstein, *Genoa and the Genoese,"* pp. 62–63. See also, Jacques Heers, *Genova nel '400*, pp. 173–305; 363–373.

154  Oscar Gelderblom, "The Governance of Early Modern Trade. The Case of Hans Thijs, 1556-1611," *Enterprise and Society*, vol. 4, no. 4, 2003, pp. 606–639. By comparing Hans Thijs's commerce with the differing scale and scope of commerce in Amsterdam and Gdansk, Gelderblom demonstrates how the best combination of governance modes materialized in Amsterdam. In fact, it was there that good infrastructural conditions (large fleets, logistics, big markets, investment capital, and availability of information), coupled with the institution of proven effectiveness in the protection of property rights, could be found.

and the relationships among networks, commercial outposts, and local authorities[155]

In short, these examples do not corroborate the idea, conveyed by the cultural-cognitive approach, that reasoning on entrepreneurship has turned into a choked alternative in post-Chandlerian business history. On the contrary, some of those works, and others in "non-revisionist" business history, remain a rich source of insights for responding to the Schumpeter plea.[156]

---

155  Ulf Christian Ewert and Stephan Selzer, *Institutions of Hanseatic Trade. Studies on the Political Economy of a Medieval Trade Organization*, Bern, Peter Lang, 2016. The two authors apply transaction costs theory in a comparative assessment of the impact of these factors as sources of competitive advantage or as constraints on business. What emerges is that the Hansa may be depicted, at least partially, as a "small work", in that the trade system worked with limited capital and vigorously attempted to protect itself from competition. Besides, the system of "reciprocal trade" did not claim any significant innovations in commercial techniques. Hence, the conclusion is that such a kind of "repeated clustered interaction of network members"-always the same people in the same cities-brings about a "network paradox" such that, at the onset of the XVI century, the competitiveness of Hansa merchants "suffered significantly during the transatlantic expansion of the European trade." (Ibid., pp. 133–135). However, an important institutions did exist in the Baltic area to support interactions between a large number of distant communities and between individual merchants, namely, the inter-communal conciliation mechanism. In case of a dispute, conciliation involved town councils, rather than the merchants involved in the dispute, thus combining individual liability and communal enforcement. See, Mika Kallioinen, "Inter-Communal Institutions in Medieval Trade," *Economic History Review*, vol. 70, no. 4, 2017, pp. 1131–1152.

156  For a research agenda outside the cultural turn see, Mark Casson and Catherine Casson, *The Entrepreneur in History. From Medieval Merchant to Modern Business Leader*, Basingstoke,

## 6.2. Another way of reasoning

In an exhaustive review of the entrepreneur as treated in economic literature, Robert Hébert and Albert Link discuss twelve forms of entrepreneurship which emerge in their chronological trace from the 18th century to the present. For the aims of the present study, two themes in their discussion appear as the most relevant: first the entrepreneur as a decision-maker who assumes the risk associated with uncertainty and second the entrepreneur as an organizer and coordinator of economic resources (possibly in the role of contractor).[157]

A definition of entrepreneurship which embraces these two overlapping themes has been provided by Arthur Cole: "… the purposeful activity [...] of an individual or group of associated individuals, undertaken to initiate, maintain, or aggrandize a profit-oriented business unit [...] within the conditions established by the internal situation of the unit itself or with [...] the institutions and practices of a period which allows an appreciable measure of freedom of decision."[158] Worth noting, in this definition, is that "purposeful activity" is taken to mean an entrepreneurial activity directed toward profit maximization, but also refer to the rational ability to make decisions and to implement them under conditions of uncertainty. And, the reference to "an integrated sequence of decisions" suggests

---

Palgrave 2013; *Idem*, "The History of Entrepreneurship: Medieval Origins of a Modern Phenomenon," *Business History*, vol. 56, no. 8, 2014, pp. 1223–1242.

157 Robert Hébert and Albert Link, "Historical Perspectives on the Entrepreneur," *Foundations and Trends in Entrepreneurship*, vol. 2, no. 4, 2006, pp. 264–265.

158 Arthur Cole, *Change and the Entrepreneur*, Cambridge, MA, Harvard University Press, 1949, quoted in, Robert Hébert and Albert Link, p. 365.

the importance of organizational structures and process in the conceptual understanding of entrepreneurship.

Besides this way of defining entrepreneurship in association with the risks and uncertainties stemming from specific environmental features, there was another way to elaborate on Schumpeter's theory in economic literature. Hebert and Link suggest a though-provoking way to compare and contrast the two perspectives. On the one hand, they refer to the idea of Ronald Coase that the best way to allocate resources along the production cycle depends on the transaction costs implied in each stage of the transfer process. When the costs of transfer via the price system of a batch of production are higher, that batch will be processed "in house"; if the contrary applies, it will be put out to one or more contractors. On the other, they recall Frank Knight and his theorization of risk and uncertainty which challenges Coase's assertion that uncertainty related to transaction costs is the only issue at stake.[159] Before coping with this kind of uncertainty, the entrepreneur must take into account the output-price uncertainty. Transaction costs come into play only after an understanding has been reached about the factors which impinge on the decision to make or buy.

Knight's point is that one should avoid taking the markets for granted. What is to be decided in advance is what good to produce and with what kind of organization, and this cannot be done by the prices (which allocate existing resources) but by the entrepreneurs. Knight's conclusion, then, is that Coase forsakes uncertainty, for he focuses on the execution of economic activities to the detriment of conception and planning. But this is the theory of the firm, which is abstract from time

---

159  Ronald Coase, "The Nature of the Firm," *Economica*, no. 4, 1937, pp. 386–405.

and uncertainty, not a theory of entrepreneurship. In Knight's view, entrepreneurs are more than contractors in that they are specialists at uncertainty bearing, and while the contract is one way to reduce uncertainty, some uncertainty can never be eliminated.[160]

On the second theme – the entrepreneurial agency as an equilibrating or disequilibrating force – Hebert and Link recall an extension of Schumpeter's concept worth thinking about. As Theodore Schultz maintains, the analysis should also encompass the rebalancing outcomes of non-market activities carried out by a set of socio-economic actors when they reallocate their resources. To this, Schultz also adds that such a widespread capacity to perceive and react to disequilibria is to be seen mainly as an outcome of the human capital garnered during the educational process. The innovative entrepreneur creates developmental disequilibria, he notes, but Schumpeter did not consider the rewards that accrue to those who bring about economic equilibration with their non-market activities. According to Schultz, the question may be tackled by remaining fully within the neoclassical paradigm while advancing with the study of entrepreneurship from the angle of human capital theory.[161]

In concluding their review, Hebert and Link point to the persistence in the literature of themes such as perception, uncertainty and innovation. They also stress how some writers follow Schumpeter in seeing the entrepreneur as a disequilibrating

---

160 Hebert and Link, "Historical Perspectives on the Entrepreneur," p. 387.
161 Theodore Schultz, "The Value of the Ability to Deal with Disequilibria," *Journal of Economic Literature*, no. 13, 1975, p. 827–846.

force while others, following Kirzner, stress how his rebalancing role materializes after some exogenous shocks.[162] In light of what emerged from the present study, I submit that new insights on how to take up the Schumpeter's plea may be drawn from both the Coase-Knight debate and some intersections of Schumpeter's and Kirzner's views of the entrepreneurs.

In his early work on market competition and entrepreneurship, Israel Kirzner deals with the entrepreneur as equilibrator in a way that subsequent readings would have crystallized as a "passive noticer of already occurred changes." In a more recent essay, Kirzner set out to dispel some previous misunderstandings to prove that his and Schumpeter's position on creativity and/ or alertness to opportunities for profit are far from mutually exclusive.[163] As he puts it, that misconception led to the wrong idea that the creative destruction of innovative entrepreneurs and the equilibrative entrepreneurial reactions to changes in the underlying supply and demand conditions are two incompatible views.[164]

In essence, the first point of Kirzner corrective clarification is that the early account of a merely-alert entrepreneur was deliberately couched in a simple analytical model whereby he abstracted from the creative and speculative element of entrepreneurship in real life. Actually, opportunities do "exist" in the real world only in a speculative sense for they can be realized only in the future. In a relevant sense, though, they are already there to be seen by the entrepreneur-arbitrageur, even if the opportunity to buy and sell at different prices will come into reality only in the future.

---

162  Hebert and Link, p. 393.
163  Israel Kirzner, "The Alert and Creative Entrepreneur: A Clarification," *IFN Working Papers*, no. 760, 2008.
164  Ibid., p. 7.

Kirzner adds that, once such a pure arbitrage element is recognized to exist, the road is open to yet another recognition – important for the Schumpeterian vision – that the innovative entrepreneur too is engaged in arbitrage. In fact, "What he "sees" is that, by assembling available resources in an innovative [...] fashion, and thus perhaps converting them into new [...] products, he may be able (in the future) to sell output at prices which exceed the cost of that output to himself". And, of course, "price differentials may occur in contexts in which the entrepreneurs who are today buying resource services, do so in order to introduce dramatically more efficient methods of production."[165]

The second important point in Kirzner's clarification is that surely, it is the prospect of profit available for the taking that inspires entrepreneurial alertness. Yet, "Public policies which to any degree deaden the excitement inspired by the prospect of pure entrepreneurial profit, must surely, lower the level of entrepreneurial alertness." Creativity is surely much more than alertness, "But the creativity that drives profit-winning entrepreneurial behavior embraces alertness too – alertness to present and future price patterns, [...] to new technological possibilities, and [...] to possible future patterns of demand. Public policies which tend to promote alertness do promote creativity as well."[166] However, the case in point also suggests some concluding thoughts for reasoning on entrepreneurship when the contrary applies to public policies as it happened in Genoa in the aftermath of the Spanish crown financial crash.

---

165 Ibid., pp. 9–10.
166 Ibid., p. 11.

# Chapter Seven     Summary and concluding remarks

This study has sketched two examples of biography in context with the aim of providing new insights into the debate on "reinventing" entrepreneurial studies in business history. The research path chosen here draws from the approaches in which biography is seen as a prism to look at events and processes in a given historical juncture. Actually, the descriptive part of the case suggested that the aim of putting a historical face on entrepreneurship is not feasible by "singularising history" through an investigation of actions and events in detail without looking outwards at the larger context.

Our "glocal" and upwardly mobile actors, born in two little adjacent communities, did not require a study limited to the boundaries of their small homeland. The focus then was on the key features of the contexts whereby their social advancement took place, and their careers took off: Genoa and its geopolitical arena. Accordingly, the analysis of the initial context drew inspiration from historical accounts of the cultural specificity and self-perception of Genoese citizens and the way it impinged on the process of institution building. In other words, the attempt was to highlight how social behaviour could be somewhat regulated – in a polity with a transactional focus – through peculiar forms of reciprocal adaptations between rule makers and rule takers who both shared the same economic culture.

The evidence from the case in point seems to justify the tenet of society conceived of as a socio-institutional system which can be changed by individuals and groups who exploit their cultural and relational resources. But the thesis must be specified by addressing further issues. What kind of cultural resources did prevail in the dual polity economy examined here? How were they put to use by economic and institutional actors similar to those depicted in the case? What was the impact on their transnational careers of the critical junctures of Genoese history of which they were witnesses? The lessons learned from the case can be summarized as follows.

First, economic culture may remain for long a major underpinning of a polity with a transactional focus until the shocks of a critical juncture trigger processes of socio-economic change which weaken and transform the ruling class that embodied the values of such a culture. That was what took place when the Spanish crown's default brought about a significant economic decline in the city-state. A decline that should have been reversed by the recurrent proposals of a new layer of politicians an intellectuals to restore Genoa's power at sea through a public fleet and a free port. Proposals which remained almost unpractical due to the scant awareness those institutional actors had of the preconditions to implement them on sea and earth.

Second, a polity with a transactional focus should be analyzed, bearing in mind structural continuities and changes in the governance on three levels: the capacity of government to enforce its policies; the dual character of Genoa's polity economy, and the vulnerability of the city-state to external shocks. These lessons from the casing process have been analytically framed by giving due attention to both the cultural and institutional features of the initial context, and the entrepreneurial agency displayed in the shifting contexts crossed by our upwardly mobile actors. Thus, in light of the two biographical outlines, the next step was to look again for conceptual and methodological insights to research works within and without (and prior to) the cultural turn. Specifically, the premises of the cultural-cognitive groundwork aimed at reinventing entrepreneurship in business history have been contrasted with the insights from some seminal works in the economic literature on the entrepreneurial role.

In the cultural turn the cognitive research premises for the study of entrepreneurship, and its impact on socio-economic and institutional change have been identified in: the temporal foundations of agency (how actors figure out a desirable future); the pursuit of extra-economic opportunities by distributed forms of human agency of various kind of social actors. The methodological implications of these guidelines materializes in a research design aimed at clarifying how opportunities are being discovered and enacted with a focus on entrepreneurial processes and not on individual and organizational action , which is, instead, the approach chosen here.

Indeed, what the case suggests is to focus our thoughts on the lifeworks of upwardly mobile and cosmopolitan individuals in a variety of contexts: the "corporate city," its state, its dominions, its merchant communities and its geopolitical space. This has been done by referring to some works that provide the best food for thought to define the entrepreneurial agency of historical actors. Two are the crucial themes in this respect: the role of entrepreneurs as risk-takers, on the one hand, and their role as equilibrating or disequilibrating forces within the economic model of general equilibrium. These two themes and the way they overlap are referred to in the Coase-Knight debate on whether or not the entrepreneur should be considered as a contractor only focused on the transaction costs of "making" in house or buying on the market. And are referred as well to Kirzner's clarification of the complementarities between his emphasis on "alertness" to profit from price differentials in buying and selling, and Schumpeter's definition of the entrepreneur as an innovator.

These two classic debates in economic literature are a good frame of reference to conceptualize the two forms of entrepreneurial agency depicted here. The first one was that of Bartolomeo da Framura, a contractor who possessed the alertness of an arbitrageur, but was also able to display the quality of a Schumpeterian entrepreneur who discovered resources and valorized them. The second was that of Gioachino da Passano who became a key institutional actor early in his lifework, but remained a skilful transactor who was able to upgrade the content and widen the context of his transactions in the wider arena of geopolitics.

The intersections of the themes of entrepreneurship as risk-taking, and as a rebalancing force may be the baseline to address our two forms of entrepreneurial agency, and to see what they suggest on the idea – in the cultural turn – to save from chocking the study of entrepreneurship in business history. On this some preliminary and concluding thoughts.

The first actor with causal capacities to come on stage was Bartolomeo da Framura whose story fits well with the theme of the entrepreneur as both a disequilibrating and rebalancing force. In fact, the evidence on the global life of this contractor corroborates one of the main points Kirzner made in his clarifying the complementarities between his and Schumpeter's concept of entrepreneurship. What we see at work in this case is an economic actor quite similar to the entrepreneur-arbitrageur who discovers in another place the same resources which provided opportunities for profit gradually abandoned in their original location due to geopolitical shocks. However, this contractor was able to rely on his institutional networking to act as an innovator as well by exploiting the new resources soon after he discovered them.

Gioachino da Passano was instead more than a contractor since the outset of his transprofessional and transnational career. To understand why and how a reference to the main antecedent of Knight's theory on the entrepreneurial risk is in order. In his classic work, Richard Cantillon saw the origins of entrepreneurship in the lack of perfect foresight individuals have about the future. Hence, those who continually cope with uncertainty in their economic decision are entrepreneurs, but not in the sense Schumpeter would subsequently give to the term. Cantillon saw the entrepreneur not as an individual who creates demand through new production or merchandising techniques. The entrepreneur he depicts is not required to display particular innovative capacities. He just needs to be alert and follow the dictates of "a class of landlords and fashion leaders" to whom he must provide goods and services at the right time and place.

The methodological implication Hebert and Link draw from this assessment of Cantillon approach is that we should focus not much on the entrepreneur's personality, as on the entrepreneurial function being performed.[167] Actually, the biographical sketch on Gioachino da Passano may be framed by this classic approach, but with some qualifications on the themes of alertness and uncertainty. This high-rank institutional actor had to be alert, but not to the dictates of a layer of landlords. He was an agent of a principal who assigned him crucial tasks in his attempt to reverse the geopolitical equilibrium of the time. He had to be persistently alerted to the gains to pursue and the losses to avoid in his political transactions. Therefore, contra Hebert and Link, the focus of analysis should not neglect the personality traits of this skilful transactor, even more so that his alertness was coupled with the ability to fix bad situations on behalf of members of the ruling class.

These were the qualities which allowed this political and institutional actor to cope with the recurring shocks in the international arena. Such a combination of personality traits made this character another example of both Schumpeterian and

---

167  Hebert e Link, pp. 280–281.

Kirznerian entrepreneur. In that capacity, he was more than a contractor insofar as he proved able to upgrade the content of his transactions in his early passage from the domain of economics to that of government in the city-state first and France later on. These were the settings whereby Gioachino da Passano displayed the qualities of a risk bearer but also of an innovator able to collect and process knowledge and information. Indeed, this key actor may be included among those entrepreneurial agents whom Hebert and Link depict as able to combine "intelligence," knowledge, and ability to act.[168]

The second point of Kirzner's clarification on the factors which impinge on alertness and creativity is also worth thinking about:

> "To be sure, creativity is much more than alertness. But the creativity that drives profit-winning entrepreneurial behavior embraces alertness too – [...] to present and future price patterns, [...] to new technological possibilities, and [...] to possible future patterns of demand. Public policies which tend to promote alertness, are policies which tend to promote creativity.[169]

But Kirzner also refers to public policies which may dull alertness and creativity. What happened in the Genoese polity economy in the period next to that considered here somewhat corroborates this statement. Admittedly, public policies in the case in point were intervening variables. The root causes of the "dullness" are to be searched in what came next in a "Century of the Genoese" bound to finish in the aftermaths of the Spanish crown financial crashes (1627–1640), The shrinking of entrepreneurial qualities was brought about by process of financialization of an economy

---

168  Ibid., p. 284.

169  Israel Kirzner, "The Alert and Creative Entrepreneur: A Clarification," *IFN Working Papers*, no. 760, 2008, pp. 11.

largely oriented toward the money lending especially toward the Spanish crown and empire.

However, the case in point has shown that those well versed in the art of shaping the future through sense-making and rhetorical processes were not as much of entrepreneurs as social actors who claimed to speak on behalf of the citizenship. For instance, during the economic downturn and decay (mid-17th century), a long-lasting rhetorical process was on display in Genoese political life regarding how the decline could be reversed with proposals for building a public fleet as was done in Venice. That long-debated issue was aptly summarized by Thomas Kirk as "Real navies, rhetorical navalism and the free port." Why? Because the many proposals advanced for decades did not contain any hints of either the kind of trade to get involved in or the possible destinations. This should not appear strange if one is aware of who the proponents were: "not merchants involved in long-distance trade but political and intellectual personalities."[170]

Thus, one can subscribe to the critique William Thornton and Patricia Ocasio addressed to an institutional theory often left adrift with previous "carrier" perspectives:

> Much of what is called institutional theory these days is not very institutional at all. Instead it is about resource dependencies, political struggles, social movements, and other mechanisms which, while important, are really about non-institutional forces driving institutional change. Within this political sociological vein, culture is relegated to the

---

170 Thomas Kirk, *Genoa and the Sea. Policy and Power in an Early Modern Maritime Republic, 1559-1684*, John Hopkins University Press, 2013, pp. 127–128.

narrower topic of how groups and social movements make use of rhetoric and framing to be persuasive. [171]

To conclude, this case study has been configured as a preliminary attempt to provide new insights for a historical reasoning on entrepreneurship on a different basis than those expounded within the cultural turn. First, the conceptualization of entrepreneurship should be pursued without muddling the concepts of culture and institutions. Instead of watering down the notion of entrepreneurship through an emphasis on the pursuit of extra-economic opportunities, a warning should be given due attention. As Oliver Williamson pointed out, culture is not *tosh*, but it should stay in its place and not be confused with institutions. The search for an approach more sensitive to agency does not necessarily imply that the socio-psychological concept of motivation should overcome that of economic incentive.[172]

Second, the transactional focus which materialized in the corporate city should be addressed without neglecting the dual nature of its polity economy in critical junctures of history. Transactions are governed not solely by the rationale of hierarchy and market. Between the two, there are intermediary governance modes to be addressed without neglecting the functional substitutes that a given bureaucracy may put in place to offset its weak capacities for enforcement

Third, a company approach should not be skipped to highlight – as far as possible – what upwardly mobile

---

171   Patricia Thornton and William Ocasio, "Institutional Logic," in Roy Greenwood et al. (eds.), *The SAGE Handbook of Organizational Institutionalism*, SAGE, 2008, p. 121.

172   Oliver Williamson, "Transaction Cost Economics and Organization Theory," in Neil Smelser and Richard Swedberg (eds.), *Handbook of Economic Sociology*, Princeton University Press, 1994, pp. 97–98.

entrepreneurial agents do and how they do it in the shifting organizational and institutional contexts they came across in their lifework.

Fourth, the choice to focus on the shaping of a proto-bourgeois urban class as the outcome of historical studies on social mobility in medieval Italy has proven its heuristic value for a historical reasoning on entrepreneurship which avoids the polarized view of innovation vs. rent-seeking.

In the end, the casing process to get to a historical reasoning on entrepreneurship may draw useful insights more in the field of political economy than in cultural-cognitive approaches. The point then is: what kind of progressive research program to refine such a reasoning? The crux of the matter has been aptly synthesized by Peter Boettke starting from one of the most disputed issues in economics: How much can the benefits of voluntary exchange be improved by the creation of governmental institutions? Such a dispute revolves around two opposite views:

> The theory of public goods, monopoly and market failure all contributed to expanding the acceptance of coercion and qualifying the presumption toward voluntarism among mainstream economists. [But] each of these arguments for qualifying the presumption have been met with counter-arguments by economists that have demonstrated that so-called public goods can actually be privately provided.[173]

The research question then revolves around the "paradox of government", that is, How can a minimal state be kept in cheek and not evolve into a "maximum state"? In his essay, Boettke rethinks a debate on this paradox in the field of political

---

173 Peter Boettke, "Anarchism as a Progressive Research Program in Political Economy," in Edward Stringham (ed.), *Anarchy, State and Public Choice*, Edward Elgar, 2005, pp. 206–220.

economy which cannot be discussed in detail here. In light of what emerged from the case in point, Buchanan's answer to that question is however worth mentioning. Within the dilemma between "anarchy" of voluntary exchange and the Leviathan, one cannot dismiss the *necessity* to establish a "protective state" able to guarantee domestic and national security along with the *desirability* of a "productive state." But with an important caveat: the expansion of the state may lead to a "redistributive state" as a source of rent-seeking. The endeavour then should be that of "escaping from anarchism to effectively constructing constitutional level constraints in government so that the protective and productive states could be established without unleashing the destructive rent-seeking tendencies of the redistributive state." In short, Boettke sees the solution to such a dilemma in two possible ways. We can keep under control our opportunistic side with a limited but effective government or – as he prefers – we can be more optimistic about the possibility that the puzzle of governance may be solved in a voluntary manner within a "natural" order of sort.

In the dual polity economy of Renaissance Genoa there was a degree of creativity in finding solutions close to one or the other side of the dilemma because that state was really minimal and weak. But Bartolomeo and Gioachino – and other proto-bourgeois actors similar to them – proved that the path toward the state and statecraft was also a matter of individual choice.

# Synopsis

The book presents two examples of biography in history analytically framed within the stream of research on social mobility in medieval and early modern Italy, and then compared with the organizational and institutional behavior of some Atlantic entrepreneurs of the sixteen century. This framework takes also into account the dualism and transactional focus of the Genoese polity with the aim of reassessing the historical reasoning on entrepreneurship proposed by business historians who responded to the "Schumpeter's plea" in this regard.

# References


Airaldi, Gabriella. *Andrea Doria*, Roma, Salerno Editrice, 2015.

Ait, Ivana. "Dal governo signorile al governo mercantile: i monti della Tolfa e le 'lumere' del papa," in *Mélanges de l'Ecole française de Rome-Moyen Age*, 126–1, 2014, pp. 1–59.

Aldrich, Howard and Martin Ruef. *Organizations Evolving*, Newbury Park SAGE, 2006.

Alonge, Guillaume. "Evangelismo e ortodossia nella diplomazia franco-turca di Francesco I," *Melanges de l'Ecole française de Rome-Italie et Mediterrannée modernes et contemporaines*, 2017, 129–2.

Andrade, Tonio. "A Chinese Farmer, Two Black Boys, and a Warlord: Towards a Global Microhistory," *The Journal of World History*, vol. 21, no. 4, 2011, pp.573-591.

Appellániz, Francisco. "Venetian Trading Networks in the Medieval Mediterranean," *Journal of Interdisciplinary History*, vol. XLIV, no. 2, 2013, pp. 157–179.

Assereto, Giovanni. *Le metamorfosi della repubblica. Saggi di storia genovese tra il XVI e il XIX secolo*, Savona, Daner, 2000.

Assereto, Giovanni. "Le vicende del Banco fra la fine del regime aristocratico e l'annessione al Regno di Sardegna," in Giuseppe Felloni (ed.), *La Casa di San Giorgio: il potere del credito*, Genova, Brigati, 2006.

Assereto, Giovanni and Giuseppe Bongiovanni. *Sotto il felice e dolce dominio della Serenissma Repubblica. L'acquisto di Finale da parte di Genova e la distinta relazione di Filippo Cattaneo De Marini*, Savona, Daner, 2003.

Aymard, Maurice. "La transizione dal feudalesimo al capitalismo," in Karol Modzelewski et al. (eds.), *Storia d'Italia. Annali I. Dal feudalesimo al capitalismo*, Torino, Einaudi, 1978, pp. 1160–1172.

Banner, Lois. "Biography as History," *American Historical Review*, vol. 114, no. 3, 2009, pp. 579–586.

Basso, Enrico. "Prima di Tolfa: i mercanti genovesi e l'allume orientale," *Melanges de l'Ecole française de Rome-Moyen Age, 126–1*, 2014.

Basso, Enrico. "La presenza genovese in Inghilterra e le relazioni commerciali anglo-genovesi nella seconda metà del XV secolo," in Marcella Arca Petrucci e Simonetta Conti (eds.), *Giovanni Caboto e le vie dell'Atlantico Settentrionale*, Roma, CISGE, 1999, pp. 17–39.

Basso, Enrico. *Insediamenti e commercio nel Mediterraneo bassomedievale: i mercanti genovesi dal Mar Nero all'Atlantico*, Torino, M. Valerio, 2008.

Baumol, William. "Entrepreneurship in Economic Theory," *Economic Review*, vol. 58, no. 2, 1968 pp. 64–71.

Beckert, Jens. "Agency, Entrepreneurs, and Institutional Change. The Role of Strategic Choice and Institutionalized Practices in Organizations," *Organization Studies*, vol. 20, no. 5, 1999, pp. 777–799.

Berghahn, Volker. "Structuralism and Biography: Some Concluding Thoughts on the Uncertainties of a Historiographical Genre," in Volker R. Berghahn and Simone Lassig (eds.), *Biography Between Structure and Agency, Central European Lives in International Historiography*, Oxford Berghahn Books, 2008, pp. 234–250.

Bernabò, Barbara. "La storia secolare di un territorio antico," in Andrea Lercari(ed.), *Frmura. Un'antica terra ligure fra il mare e I monti,* Genova, AGF, 2017, pp. 265–332.

Bitossi, Carlo. 'L'età di Andrea Doria', pp. 61–78 in, *Storia della Liguria,* a cura di Giovanni Assereto e Marco. Doria, Laterza, Bari, 2007.

Bitossi, Carlo. *"La Repubblica di Genova: politica e istituzioni,"* pp. 79–97 in, Giovanni Assereto and Marco Doria (eds.), *Storia della Liguria,* Bari, Laterza, 2007.

Boettke, Peter. "Anarchism as a Progressive Research Program in Political Economy," in Edward Stringham (ed.), *Anarchy, State and Public Choice,* Cheltenham Edward Elgar, 2005, pp. 206–220.

Boettke, Peter and Christopher Coyne. "Context Matter: Institutions and Entrepreneurship," *Foundations and Trends in Entrepreneurship,* vol. 5, no. 3, 2009, pp. 135–209.

Bourdieu, Pierre. "The Forms of Capitalism," in John Richardson (ed.), *Handbook of Theory and Research for the Sociology of Education,* Westport, Greenwood, 1986.

Bravo Lozano, Cristina, Roberto Quirós Rosado (eds.), *En Tierra de Confluencias. Italia y la Monarquia de España,* Valencia, Albatros, 2013.

Brucker, Gene. "Tales of Two Cities: Florence and Venice in the Renaissance Italy," *The American Historical Review,* vol. 88, no. 3, 1983, pp. 599–616.

Cahen, Claude. "L'alun avant Phocée. Un chapitre d'histoire économique islamo-chrétienne au temp de Croisades," *Revue d'Histoire économique et sociale,* vol. 41, no. 4, 1963, pp. 433–447.

Caine, Barbara. *Biography and History (Theory and History)*, Basingstoke, Palgrave Macmillan, 2018.

Calcagno, Paolo, "La lotta al contrabbando nel mare Ligustico in età moderna," *Mediterranea*, vol. VII, no. 20, pp. 479–532.

Cammarosano, Paolo. "Il ricambio e l'evoluzione dei ceti dirigenti nel corso del XIII secolo," in *Magnati e popolani nell'Italia comunale*, Atti del XV Convegno di studi, Pistoia, 15–18 maggio 1995, pp. 17–40, 1997.

Carlos, Ann and Stephen Nicholas. "Giants of an Earlier Capitalism: The Chartered Trading Companies as Modern Multinational," *Business History Review*, vol. LXII, 1988, pp. 398–419.

Carlos, Ann and Nicholas. "Agency Problems in Early Chartered Companies: The Case of the Hudson Bay Company," *The Journal of Economic History*, vol. 50 no. 4, 1990, pp. 853–875.

Carocci, Sandro (ed.). *La mobilità sociale nel medioevo*, Roma, Viella, 2010.

Carocci, Sandro and Isabella Lazzarini (eds.). *Social Mobility in Medieval (Italy 1100–1500)*, Roma, Viella, 2017.

Casanova, Giorgio. "Framura e il mare: una vocazione millenaria tra pescatori, naviganti e corsari," in Andrea Lercari (ed.), *Framura. Un'antica terra ligure fra il mare e I monti*, Genova, AGF, 2017.

Casini, Matteo. "Fra città-stato e Stato regionale: riflessioni politiche sullo stato della Repubblica di Venezia in età moderna," *Studi Veneziani*, XLIV, 2002, pp. 15–36.

Casson, Mark and Catherine Casson. *The Entrepreneur in History. From Medieval Merchant to Modern Business Leader*, Basingstoke, Palgrave 2013.

Casson, Mark and Catherine Casson. "The History of Entrepreneurship: Medieval Origins of a Modern Phenomenon," *Business History*, vol. 56, no. 8, 2014, pp. 1223–1242.

Chandler, Alfred. *Strategy and Structure: Chapters in the History of the Industrial Empire*, Boston, MIT Press, 1962.

Chandler, Alfred. *Scale and Scope: The Dynamics of Industrial Capitalism*, Cambridge Ma., Belknap Press, 1990.

Cipolla, Carlo M. *Storia economica dell'Europa preindustriale*, Il Bologna, Mulino, 2002.

Collavini, Simone and Giuseppe Petralia (eds.). *La mobilità sociale nel Medioevo italiano. Cambiamento economico e dinamiche sociali* (secoli XI-XV), Roma, Viella, 2020.

Degrassi, Donata. "Il mondo dei mestieri artigianali," in Sandro Carocci (ed.), *La mobilità sociale nel medioevo*, Roma, Viella, 2010, pp. 273–287.

Degrassi, Donata. "L'impresa mineraria nel Medioevo: competenze tecniche, organizzazione, mobilità geografica e sociale," in Lorenzo Tanzini and Sergio Tognetti, *La mobilità sociale nel Medioevo italiano*, Roma, Viella, 2016, pp. 25–49.

Delumeau, Jan. *Vie economique et social de Rome dans la seconde moitié du XVIe siècle*, Paris, De Boccard, 1959.

Delumeau, Jean. *L'alun de Rome. XV-XIXe siècle*, Paris, S.E.V.P.E.N., 1962.

De Vito Christian and Anne Geritsen (eds.). *Micro-Spatial Histories of Global Labour*, Basingstoke, Palgrave Macmillan, 2018.

de Vries, Jan. "Changing the Narrative: The New History That Was and Is to Come," *Journal of Interdisciplinary History*, vol. 48, no. 3, 2017, pp. 313–334.

de Vries, Jan. "Playing with Scale: The Global and the Micro, the Macro and the Nano," *Past and Present*, vol. 42, issue supplement 14, 2019, pp. 23–36.

Dimov, Dino. "Grappling with the Unbearable Elusiveness of Entrepreneurial Opportunities," *Entrepreneurship Theory and Practice*, vol. 35, no. 1, 2011, pp. 57–81.

Ebner, Alexander. "Entrepreneurship and Economic Development. From Classic Political Economy to Economic Sociology," *Journal of Economic Studies*, vol. 32, no. 3, 2005, pp. 256–274.

Eptstein, Steven. *Genoa and the Genoese, 958–1528*, Chapel Hill, University of Carolina Press, 1996.

Espinosa Aurelio. "The Grand Strategy of Charles V (1500–1558). Castile, War, and Dynastic Priority in the Mediterranean," *Journal of Early Modern History*, vol. 9, no. 3–4, 2005, pp. 239–283.

Esposito, Anna. "La pratica delle compagnie d'uffici alla corte di Roma tra fine '400 e inizio '500," in Armand Jamme and Olivier Poncet, *Offices, écrits et papauté (XIIIe-XVIIe siècle)*, Publication de l'Ecole française de Rome, 2007, pp. 497–515.

Ewert, Ulf Christian and Stephan Selzer. *Institutions of Hanseatic Trade. Studies on the Political Economy of a Medieval Trade Organization*, Bern, Peter Lang, 2016.

Felloni, Giuseppe. "I molteplici di Gioachino da Passano," in Lercari, *Tra grande patriziato e notabilato locale*, vol. II, 2009–2011, pp. 645–666.

Felloni, Giuseppe. *A Profile of Genoa's Casa di San Giorgio (1407–1805): A Turning Point in the History of Credit*, in Rivista di Storia Economica, no. 3, 2010, pp. 335–346.

Gamberini, Andrea (ed.), *La mobilità sociale nel Medioevo italiano. Stato e istituzioni (secoli XIV-XV)*, Roma, Viella, 2017.

Garnier, Edith. *Guillaume du Bellay. L'ange gardien de François Ier*, Paris, Du Felin, 2016.

Garud, Raghu, Cynthia Hardy and Steve Maguire. "Institutional Entrepreneurship as Embedded Agency: An Introduction to the Special Issue," *Organization Studies*, vol. 28, no. 7, 2007, pp. 1–14.

Gelderblom, Oscar. "The Governance of Early Modern Trade. The Case of Hans Thijs, 1556–1611," *Enterprise and Society*, vol. 4, no. 4, 2003, pp. 606–639.

George, Alexander and Andrew Bennet, *Case Studies and Theory Development in the Social Science*, Boston, MIT Press, 2005.

Gerschenkron, Alexander. *Economic Backwardness in Historical Perspective*, Cambridge Ma., Harvard University Press, 1962.

Geyskens, Inge, Jan Steenkamp and Nyrmalya Kumar. "Make, Buy, or Ally: A Transaction Cost Theory Meta-Analysis," p. 521, *Academy of Management Journal*, vol. 49, no. 3, 2006, pp. 519–543.

Ginsburg, Carlo. *Il formaggio e i vermi*, Torino, Einaudi, 1976.

Ginsburg, Carlo. "Microhistory: Two or Three Things That I Know About It," *Critical Inquiry*, vol. 10, no. 1, 1993, pp. 10–35.

Goffman, Daniel. *The Ottoman Empire and Early Modern Europe*, Cambridge University Press, 2004.

Grancelli, Bruno. *Nobili, mercanti e navigatori framuresi. Azione economica, arte, diplomazia nel Secolo dei Genovesi*, Carrara, Impressum, 2019.

Greif, Avner. *Institutions and the Path to the Modern Economy. Lessons from Medieval Trade*, Cambridge University Press, 2006.

Grendi, Edoardo. *La repubblica aristocratica dei genovesi*, Bologna, Il Mulino, 1987.

Grendi, Edoardo. *Il Cervo e la repubblica. Il modello ligure di antico regime*, Torino, Einaudi, 1993.

Grendi, Edoardo. "Ripensare la microstoria?" *Quaderni Storici*, vol. 29, no. 86, 1994, pp. 539–549.

Grossi Bianchi, Luciano and Ennio Poleggi. *Una città portuale nel medioevo: Genova nei secoli X-XVI*, Genova, SAGEP, 1987.

Guidi Bruscoli, Francesco. "Mercanti-banchieri e appalti pontifici nella prima metà del Cinquecento," in Armand Jamme and Olivier Poncet, *Offices, écrits et papauté (XIIIe XVIIe siècles)*, Publications de l'Ecole française de Rome, 2007.

Hanlon, Gregory. *Human Nature in Rural Tuscany. An Early Modern History*, Basingstoke, Palgrave MacMillan, 2015.

Hébert Robert and Albert Link, "Historical Perspectives on the Entrepreneur," *Foundations and Trends in Entrepreneurship*, vol. 2, no. 4, 2006, pp. 261–408.

Heers, Jacques. *Genova nel '400. Civiltà mediterranea, grande capitalismo e capitalismo popolare*, Milano, Jaca Book, 1983.

Henrekson, Magnus and Robin Douhan. *The Political Economy of Entrepreneurship*, Chentelham, Edward Elgar, 2008.

Hess, C. Andrew, *The Forgotten Frontier. A History of the Sixteenth-Century Forgotten Ibero-African Frontier*, The University of Chicago Press, 2010.

Hodgson, Geoffrey. *How Economics Forgot History: The Problem of Historical Specificity in Social Science*, London, Routledge, 2001.

Hoover, Calvin. "The Sea Loan in Genoa in the Twelfth Century," *The Quarterly Journal of Economics*, vol. 40, no. 3, 1926, pp. 495–529, https://doi.org/10.2307/1885175.

Jones, S. R. H. and Simon P. Ville. "Efficient Transactors or Rent-Seeking Monopolists? The Rationale for Early Chartered Trading Companies," *The Journal of Economic History*, vol. LVI, 1996, pp. 898–915.

Jones, Geoffrey and Daniel Wadhwani. "Entrepreneurship and Business History: Renewing the Research Agenda," *Harvard Business School Working Paper* no. 07–007, 2006, pp. 1–49.

Jones, Geoffrey and Daniel Wadhwani, "Entrepreneurial Theory and the History of Globalization," *Business and Economic History On-Line*, vol. 5, 2007, pp. 1–26.

Jonsson, Ivar. *The Political Economy of Innovation and Entrepreneurship. From Theories to Practice*, Chesterfield, Ashgate, 2015.

Kallioinen, Mika. "Inter-Communal Institutions in Medieval Trade," *Economic History Review*, vol. 70, no. 4, 2017, pp. 1131–1152.

Kessler-Harris, Alice. "Why Biography?" *American Historical Review*, vol. 114, no. 3, 2009, pp. 625–630.

Khvalkov, Alexandrovitch, Ievgen. *The Colonies of Genoa in the Black Sea Region: Evolution and Transformation*, Degree Thesis, European University Institute, Florence, Department of History and Civilization, 2015.

Kipping, Mathias, Takafumi Kurosawa and Daniel Wadhwani, "A Revisionist Historiography of Business History: A Richest Past for a Richer Future," in John Wilson, Steven Toms, Abe de Jong, and Emily Buchnea (eds.), *The Routledge Companion to Business History*, London, Routledge, 2017, pp. 19–35.

Kirk, Thomas. *Genoa and the Sea. Policy and Power in an Early Modern Maritime Republic, 1559–1684*, Baltimore, John Hopkins University Press, 2013.

Kirzner, Israel. "The Alert and Creative Entrepreneur: A Clarification," IFN Working Papers, No. 760, http://hdl.han dle.net/10419/81491.

Knight, Frank. *Risk, Uncertainty and Profit*, New York, Dover Publications, 2006 [1921].

Kressel, Richard. *The administration of Caffa under the Uffizio di San Giorgio*, Madison, University of Wisconsin, 1966.

Law John, *Venice and the Veneto in the Early Renaissance*, London, Routledge, 2000.

Lazzerini Isabella, "Mercatura e diplomazia: itinerari di mobilità sociale nelle élite italiane (qualche esempio fiorentino, XV secolo)," in Tanzini e Tognetti, *La mobilità sociale nel medioevo*, Viella, 2016, pp. 273–297.

Lercari, Andrea. "Una comunità ligure di antico regime: personaggi e famiglie framuresi tra XV e XVIII secolo, " pp. 265–646, in A. Lercari (ed.), *Framura. Un'antica terra ligure fra il mare e i monti*, Genova, AGF, 2017.

Lercari, Andrea (ed.). I signori da Passano. Identità territoriale, grande politica e cultura europea nella storia di una antica stirpe del Levante ligure, vol. I and II, *Giornale Storico della Lunigiana e del Territorio Lucense*, La Spezia, Edizioni Giacchè, 2009–2011.

Levi, Giovanni. "Les usages de la biographie," in *Annales E.S.C.*, vol. 44, no. 6, 1989, pp. 1325–1336.

Levi, Giovanni. "Microhistory and the Recovery of Complexity," in Susanna Fellman and Saja Rahikainen (eds.), *Historical*

*Knowledge: In Quest of Theory, Methods and Evidence*, Cambridge Scholars Publishing, 2012.

Levi, Giovanni, *L'eredità immateriale. Carriera di un esorcista nel Piemonte del Seicento*, Milano, Il Saggiatore, [1985] 2020.

Loriga, Sabina. "Negli interstizi della storia," in Paola Lanaro (ed.), *Microstoria. A venticinque anni da L'eredità immateriale*, Milano, Franco Angeli, 2011.

Loriga, Sabina. "The Plurality of the Past: Historical Time and the Rediscovery of Biography," in Hans Renders et al. (eds.), *The Biographical Turn. Lives in History*, London, Routledge, 2017, pp. 31–41.

Lopez, Roberto. *La rivoluzione commerciale nel Medioevo*, Torino, Einaudi, 1975.

Lopez, Roberto. *Storia delle colonie genovesi nel Mediterraneo*, Torino, Marietti, 1996 [1938].

Lopez, Roberto. *Benedetto Zaccaria: ammiraglio e mercante nella Genova del Duecento*. Genova, Frilli, 2004 [1933].

Lounsbury Michael and Mary Ann Glynn, *Cultural Entrepreneurship: A New Agenda for the Study of Entrepreneurial Processes and Possibilities*, Cambridge University Press, 2019.

Luongo, Alberto. "Notariato e mobilità sociale nell'Italia cittadina del XIV secolo," in Tanzini and Tognetti, *La mobilità sociale nel medioevo* italiano, 2016, pp. 243–272.

Machiavelli, Nicolò. *Istorie fiorentine*, Milano, Feltrinelli, 1962.

Marechaux, Benoit. "Business Organization in the Mediterranean Sea: Genoese Galley Entrepreneurs in the Service of the Spanish Empire (Late Sixteenth and Early Seventeenth Centuries)", *Business History*, Published on line: 10 August 2020.

McMullen, Jeffrey, Kathrina Brownell and Joel Adams, "What Makes an Entrepreneurship Study More Entrepreneurial? Toward a Unified Theory of Entrepreneurial Agency," *Entrepreneurship Theory and Practice*, vol. 45, May 2020, pp. 1197–1238.

Meister, Daniel, "The Biographical Turn and the Case for Historical Biography," *History Compass*, 2017, pp. 1–10, https://doi.org/10.1111/hic3.12436.

Mitler, Louis. "The Genoese in Galata: 1453–1682," *International Journal of Middle East Studies*, vol. 10, no. 1, 1979, pp. 71–91.

Musso, Giangiacomo. "Il tramonto di Caffa genovese," in *Miscellanea di storia ligure in memoria di Giorgio Falco*, Genova, Fonti e Studi, 1966, pp. 311–339.

Musso, Riccardo. ""El stato nostro de Zenoa." Aspetti istituzionali della prima dominazione sforzesca su Genova (1464–78)," *Serta Antiqua et Medioevalia*, no. 5, 2014, pp. 199–236.

Musso, Riccardo. "La tirannia dei *cappellazzi*," in Giovanni Assereto e Marco Doria, (eds.), *Storia della Liguria*, Bari, Laterza, 2007, pp. 47–60.

Musso, Riccardo. "Le fazioni nel medio Levante ligure tra XV e XVI secolo," in Giuliana Algeri and Valeria Polonio (eds.), *L'Oratorio dei disciplinanti di Moneglia. Testimonianza di fede e di arte nella storia di una comunità*, Atti del Convegno, Moneglia, 10–11 ottobre 2008, pp. 89–118.

Olgiati, Giustina. "The Genoese Colonies in Front of the Turkish Advance (1453–1475)," *Tarih Araştirmalari Dergisi*, vol. 15, no. 26, 1991, pp. 381–389, https://dergipark.org.tr.

Ortalli, Gherardo and Dino Puncuh (eds.), "Genova, Venezia, il Levante nei secoli XII-XIV," Genova, *Atti della Società Ligure di Storia Patria*, vol. XLI, (CXV), fasc. 1, 2000, pp. 1–17.

Pacini, Arturo. "I presupposti politici del secolo dei genovesi: la riforma del 1528," *Atti della Società Ligure di Storia Patria*, XXX, 1, 1990.

Pacini, Arturo. *La Genova di Andrea Doria nell'impero di Carlo V*, Firenze, Olschki, , 1999.

Padgett, John and Christopher Ansell. "Robust Action and the Rise of the Medici, 1400–1434," *American Journal of Sociology*, vol. 98, no. 6, 1993, pp. 1259–1319.

Padgett, John and Paul MacLean. "Organizational Invention and Elite Transformation: The Birth of Partnership Systems in Renaissance Florence," *American Journal of Sociology*, vol. 111, no. 5, 2006, pp. 1463–1568.

Panter, Sarah, Johannes Paulmann and Margit Szöllösi-Janze, "Mobility and Biography: Methodological Challenges and Perspectives," pp. 1–14 *Jahrbuch für Europäische Geschichte / European History Yearbook* –Sarah Panter, (ed.), *Band 16. Mobility and Biography*, Berlin, de Gruyter, 2015.

Peltonen, Matti. "Clues, Margins and Monads: The Micro-Macro Link in Historical Research," *History and Theory*, XL, 2001, pp. 349–351.

Pernu, Elina. "The Process of Casing in Business Studies –The Impact of Researcher's Sense Making," *Third Annual IMP Conference*, KEDGE Business School, Bordeux, Sept. 6, 2014, pp. 1–13, www.impgroup.org.

Pirenne, Henri. *Storia economica e sociale del Medioevo*, Milano, Garzanti, 1975 [1963].

Pistarino, Geo. "The Genoese in Pera – Turkish Galata," *Mediterranean Historical Review*, vol. 1, no. 1, 1986, pp. 63–85.

Pizzorno, Diego. *Genova e Roma fra Cinque e Seicento. Gruppi di potere, rapporti diplomatici, strategie internazionali*, Modena, Mucchi Editore, 2018.

Procacci, Giuliano. *Storia degli Italiani*, Bari, Laterza, 1968.

Raggio, Osvaldo. *Faide e parentele. Lo stato genovese visto dalla Fontanabuona*, Torino, Einaudi, 1990.

Renders, Hans, Binne de Haan and Jonne Harmsma. "The Biographical Turn. Biography as Critical Method in the Humanities and in Society," p. 4, in *The Biographical Turn. Lives in History*, London, Routledge, 2017, pp. 1–11.

Rohan, Padraic. *The Genoese Levantine Colonies at the Birth of Ottoman Imperial Power: A Framework for Enquiry*, Master's degree thesis, Graduate School of Social Science, Istanbul Şehir University, 2015, p. 1–113. https://core.ac.uk.

Rotschild, Emma. *The Inner Life of Empires-An Eighteenth Century History*, Princeton University Press, 2011.

Salonia, Matteo. *Genoa's Freedom. Entrepreneurship, Republicanism, and the Spanish Atlantic*, Lanham, Lexington Books, 2017.

Sánchez, Herrero, Manuel. "El modelo repubblicano en una monarquía de ciudades," pp. 245–266, in Hugon, Alain and Alexandra Merle (eds.), *Soulèvements, Révoltes, Révolutions*, Madrid, Casa de Velázques, 2017.

Sanchez, Herrero, Manuel, Garcia Ben Yessef, Yasmina Rocio, Carlo Bitossi and Dino Puncuh (eds.), *Génova y la Monarquia Hispánica (1528–1713)*, Genova, Atti della Società Ligure di Storia Patria, vol. LI (CXXV), fasc. 1, 2011.

Saraceno, Pietro. "L'amministrazione delle colonie genovesi nell'area del Mar Nero dal 1261 al 1453." *Rivista di Storia del Diritto Italiano* 42/43, 1969, pp. 177–226.

Savelli, Rodolfo. *La Repubblica oligarchica. Legislazione, istituzioni e ceti sociali a Genova nel Cinquecento*, Milano, Giuffré, 1981.

Selznick, Philip. *TVA and the Grass Roots. A Study in the Sociology of Formal Organizations*, Berkeley, University of California Press, 1949.

Selznick, Philip. *The Organizational Weapon: A Study of Bolshevik Strategy and Tactics*, New York, McGraw-Hill, 1952.

Seo Myeong-Gu and Douglas Creed. "Institutional Contradictions, Praxis, and Institutional Change: A Dialectic Perspective," *Academy of Management Review*, 27, 2002 pp. 222–247.

Shaw, Christine. "Principles and Practice of Civic Government of Fifteenth-Century Genoa," *Renaissance Quarterly*, vol. 58, no. 1, 2005, pp. 45–90.

Shubert, Adrian. "What Do Historians Really Think about Biography," *Letras de Hoje*, vol. 53, no. 2, 2018, pp. 96–102.

Sieveking, Heinrich. *Studio sulle finanze genovesi nel Medioevo*, Genova, Associazione Ligure di Storia Patria, 35, vol. I, 1905 and vol. II, 1906.

Sorokin, Pitirim A. *Social Mobility*, London, Routledge Thoemmes Press, 1998 [1927].

Strangio, Donatella. "Public Debt in the Papal States, Sixteenth to Eighteenth Century," *Journal of Interdisciplinary History*, vol. 43, no. 4, 2013, pp.511-537.

Tanzini, Lorenzo e Sergio Tognetti. *La mobilità sociale nel Medioevo italiano. Competenze, conoscenze e saperi tra professioni e ruoli sociali* (secc. XII-XV), Roma, Viella, 2016.

Thornton, Patricia. "The Sociology of Entrepreneurship," *Annual Review of Sociology*, no. 25, 1999, pp. 19–46.

Thornton Patricia and William Ocasio, Institutional Logic, in Roy Greenwood et al. *The SAGE Handbook of Organizational Institutionalism*, Newbury Park, SAGE, 2008.

Tigrino, Vittorio. "Il dibattito storico-politico sul Dominio della Repubblica di Genova in età moderna: feudi, ex-feudi, città e quasi-città," in *Libertà e dominio*, (undated), Ricerche DHL, 6, bozza 1, pp. 315–66.

Tognetti, Sergio. "Uomini d'affari e mobilità sociale in Italia tra metà Trecento e primo Cinquecento," *Estratto da Archivio Storico Italiano*, 1–a. 175 no. 651, Firenze, Olschki, 2017, pp. 119–150.

Trivellato, Francesca. *The Familiarity of Strangers: The Sephardic Diaspora, Livorno and Cross-Cultural Trade in the Early Modern Period*, New Haven, Yale University Press, 2009.

Trivellato, Francesca. "Is There a Future for Italian Microhistory in the Age of Global History?" *California Italian Studies*, vol. 2, no. 1, 2011, http://dx.doi.org/10.5070/C321009025.

Tuchman, Barbara, "Biography as a Prism of History," in Marc Pachter (ed.), *Telling Lives: The Biographer's Art*, Philadelphia, University of Pennsylvania Press, 1981, pp. 133–147.

Van Doosselaere, Quentin. *Commercial Agreements and Social Dynamics in Medieval Genoa*, Cambridge University Press, 2009, pp. 14–17.

Venesson, Pascal. "Case Studies and Process Tracing: Theories and Practices," in Donatella della Porta and Michael Keating (eds.), *Approaches and Methodologies in the Social Sciences: A Pluralist Perspective*, Cambridge University Press, 2008, pp. 223–239.

Wadhwani, Daniel and Christina Lubinski. "Reinventing Entrepreneurial History," *Business History Review*, vol. 91 (Winter 2017), pp. 767–799.

Wadhwani, Daniel. "Entrepreneurship in Historical Context: Using History to Develop Theory and Understand Process," in Friederike Welter and Bill Gartner (eds.), *A Research Agenda for Entrepreneurship and Context*, Cheltenham, Edward Elgar, 2016, pp. 65–78.

Wadhwani, Daniel and Geoffrey Jones. "Schumpeter's Plea: Historical Reasoning in Entrepreneurship Theory and Research," in Marcelo Bucheli and Daniel Wadhwani (eds.), *Organizations in Time: History, Theory and Methods*, Oxford University Press, 2014, pp. 192–216.

Weber Benjamin. "Lutter contre le Turcs: Les formes nouvelles de la croisade pontificale au XVe siecle (l'alun de Tolfa)," *Collection de l'Ecole française de Rome*, no. 42, 2013, pp. 315–324.

Welter Friederike and William B. Gartner (eds.), *A Research Agenda for Entrepreneurship and Context*, Cheltenham, Edward Elgar, 2016.

Williamson, Oliver. "The Evolving Science of Organization," *Journal of Institutional and Theoretical Economics*, vol. 149, no. 1, 1993, pp. 36–63.

Williamson, Oliver. "Transaction Cost Economics and Organization Theory," in Neil J. Smelser and Richard

Swedberg (eds.), *Handbook of Economic Sociology*, Princeton University Press, 1994, pp. 77–107.

Williamson, Oliver. "The New Institutional Economics: Taking Stock, Looking Ahead," *Journal of Economic Literature*, vol. 38, no. 3, 2000, pp. 595–613.

Wirta, Kaarle. "Rediscovering Agency in the Atlantic. A Biographical Approach Linking Entrepreneurial Spirit and Overseas Companies," in Hans Renders, Binne de Haan and Jonne Harmsma (eds.), *The Biographical Turn: Lives in History*, London, Routledges, 2017, pp. 118–129.

Wirta, Kaarle. *Early Modern Overseas Trade and Entrepreneurship: Nordic Trading Companies in the Seventeenth Century*, London, Routledge, 2020.

Yasanoff, Maya. *The Dawn Watch. Joseph Conrad in a Global World*, London, Penguin, 2017.

Yun Casalilla, Bartolomé. *Las Redes del Imperio. Elites sociales en la articulación de la Monarquía Hispánica, 1492–1714*, Madrid, Marcial Pons Historia, 2009.

Zanini, Andrea. "Strategie politiche ed economia feudale ai confini della Repubblica di Genova (secoli XVI-XVIII)," Genova, *Atti della Società ligure di storia patria*, XLV-CXIX, 2005.

Zorzi, Andrea. "Il dominio territoriale di Firenze nei secoli XIV-XV: mediazioni, negoziazioni, pattuizioni, " in Francois Foronda (ed.), *Avant le contract social. Le contract politique dans l'Occident médiéval, XIIIe-XVe siecle*, pp. 81–96, Paris, Editions de la Sorbonne, 2011.